Advance Praise for
Jesus and Therapy

"Between her unabashed willingness to delineate the
unseen depths of trauma, mental health, and faith,
and her writing that is all at once visceral, relatable,
and witty, Tabitha is a true rarity. Her words are the
unspoken truths of millions."

> —Sophia San Filippo, managing editor of
> *Love What Matters*

"Tabitha has been gifted with a talent of articulating
not only what so many yearn to hear, but also what
they *need* to hear. She couples love with brutal
honesty, sharing such unique circumstances in life
that, I know, are saving people around the globe.
Her words are truly resonating with countless people
while God uses her to share His grace and goodness."

> —Regan Long, co-founder of The Real Deal
> of Parenting, public speaker, and author of
> *Stuck at 5 CM, A Letter for Every Mother,*
> and *101 Moments of Motherhood*

"The Bible tells us that we will have trouble in life,
but mental illness is something many Christians
feel they should be able to overcome with faith,
causing them to question their belief system when
they cannot do so. *Jesus and Therapy* offers a fresh
and practical way to address mental illness without
shame by offering readers solutions to these struggles
as they lean on Jesus for their hope."

> —Quinn Kelly, licensed marriage and family
> therapist and host of the *Renew You* podcast
> on Air 1 & K-Love Radio

"As a mama who struggles with an anxiety disorder myself, I know how isolating and painful it can be to silently battle our own thoughts. Tabitha offers a sense of community and the affirmation that God is working and is close to us, even in the *hardest hard*."

—Jaclyn Warren, founder of *Mommy's 15 Minutes* and contributing author of *So God Made a Mother*

"For those hanging on by a thread, feeling alone and lost in the darkness of their struggles with anxiety and depression, Tabitha can relate. She uses her story in a powerful way to throw out a rope of hope to those in desperate need. This resource is one the church will be able to add to their libraries, small groups, and life-changing ministries to help believers who are depressed walk their road of restoration and healing."

—Caris Snider, speaker, podcaster, and author of the *Anxiety Elephants* series and *Car Line Mom: 100 Days of Encouragement*

"Tabitha's words are such a light to those who are hurting. She shares authentically and vulnerably from her own trials and experiences and gives hope to those who are walking through their own set of hard times. Her writing is powerful, yet real and relatable, reminding all of us that even in pain and suffering, there is still hope."

—Allison Brost, Christian singer/songwriter and author of *This Side of Perfect* and *Grateful: 30 Days of Growing in Thankfulness*

"This thoughtful and compassionate book is for anyone who has felt like an unfit or second-class Christian due to mental health stigmatization from the Christian community. Tabitha has written a deeply personal story that invites the reader into the truth about oneself (valued beyond words by Jesus) and the possibility of healing. The sections titled "Jesus and Therapy" can easily be integrated into therapy with clients who may be struggling with their faith, painful church experiences, and spiritual abuse. Tabitha is a clear, strong voice of advocacy for mental health in the church just when it is needed most."

—Michelle Caulk, PhD, licensed counselor; Director of Clinical Experiences at Huntington University; Master Accelerated Resolution Therapy (ART) Clinician; and co-author of *Healing Out Loud: How to Embrace God's Love When You Don't Like Yourself*

"We all walk through life hoping to be seen and embraced. That's especially true during times when our mental health is at its most vulnerable. But what happens when we turn to the most sacred place on earth, our church, for support and find we're neither seen nor embraced? Tabitha Yates tackles this exact harrowing period from experience, sharing her beautiful, courageous story of how she found the light after feeling abandoned and alone at her greatest time of need. If you've ever been left out by your faith leaders or Christian friends in your darkest hours, *Jesus and Therapy* will give you hope to believe once again."

—Lisa Leshaw, clinical mental health counselor and public speaker

Jesus
and
Therapy

Bridging the Gap
Between Faith and
Mental Health

Jesus
and
Therapy

Bridging the Gap
Between Faith and
Mental Health

Tabitha Yates

DEXTERITY
NASHVILLE

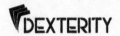
DEXTERITY

604 Magnolia Lane
Nashville, TN 37211

The information provided in this book is for educational and informational purposes only. It is not intended to serve as medical or psychological advice, diagnosis, or treatment. Readers should consult with a qualified healthcare provider or mental health professional for advice and treatment if needed.

Printed in the United States of America.

First edition: 2025
10 9 8 7 6 5 4 3 2 1

ISBN: 978-1-947297-92-0 (Paperback)
ISBN: 978-1-947297-93-7 (E-book)

Publisher's Cataloging-in-Publication Data

Names: Yates, Tabitha, author.
Title: Jesus and therapy : bridging the gap between faith and mental health / Tabitha Yates.
Description: Includes bibliographical references. | Nashville, TN: Dexterity, 2024.
Identifiers: ISBN: 978-1-947297-92-0 (paperback) | 978-1-947297-93-7 (ebook)
Subjects: LCSH Psychotherapy–Religious aspects–Christianity. | Psychotherapy patients–Religious life. |
Depressed persons–Religious life. | Depression, Mental–Religious aspects–Christianity. | BISAC RELIGION / Christian Living / General | RELIGION / Counseling | SELF-HELP / Mood Disorders / Depression
Classification: LCC BR115.C69 .Y27 2024 | DDC 261.5/15–dc23

Cover design by Thinkpen Design

Contents

A Note to Readers

Hello, friend! Thank you for picking up this book. I'm so grateful for the privilege I have been given to play a small role in your or your loved one's journey as you navigate the sometimes confusing intersection where your faith and mental health meet. Speaking of journeys, the one I've walked through to get to this moment where I'm able to witness my life come full circle could only be the result of the goodness of a God who loves a good comeback story and has an ultimate redemptive purpose in mind for even the darkest moments in life.

My story has been in the making for nearly forty years. Though shame has kept me quiet for much of my life, I'm no longer willing to stay silent. Throughout this book, I share my truth regarding the abuse and mistreatment that occurred behind closed doors, both at home and within the church, with the hope that it will be the catalyst to help you share your own story and find healing.

If I had to venture a guess as to why you picked up this book, I would say perhaps it's because you're wrestling with your mental health. Maybe you have been struggling for as long as you can remember. You haven't given up hope that your life amounts to so much more than your diagnosis. You refuse to believe that the brokenness you are facing right now is how your story ends. You might even be desperately clinging to your faith, despite possibly feeling betrayed by your Maker due to harm caused by His children. Or maybe you're struggling to find your place in the Christian community after they defined you and your faith by your mental health struggles. Perhaps believers even placed the blame for your battle at your feet—"God is punishing you." "He is trying to teach you a lesson." "Your faith is too weak." "If you prayed more, you wouldn't need antidepressants." "If you really trusted God, you wouldn't have anxiety."

Or perhaps you know someone who's in the trenches of their own battle. You've tried to help your loved one with their struggle, but you second-guess if you're saying the right thing, doing the right thing. You seek to understand the issue of mental health so that you can better support the people you care about.

The messages you will find in this book are for everyone. If you are personally struggling, I believe you will feel seen, understood, and less alone by the end of this book. If you know someone or love someone who wrestles with their mental health, you will gain tremendous knowledge, advice, and resources for how to best love and show up for that person.

Damaging perspectives about mental health challenges within the bounds of Christianity may have already led you to walk away from organized religion, the church, or perhaps even your relationship with God. After all, how loving could God be when His children, who are supposed to reflect Him, meet suffering with rejection and further wounding?

This broken spot is exactly where I found myself in my adolescent years. A home life consisting of physical, emotional, and verbal abuse had set the stage for spiritual abuse by male leadership in a cult-like fundamentalist Christian church that my family attended. Eventually, after years of abuse, pain, and abandonment, I walked away from the only God my church had ever shown me, defeated, disillusioned, and done with religion. Soon after that, at the age of sixteen, I landed in a psych ward.

I share this because I want you to understand that I know how it feels to walk out of a church and vow to never darken its doorstep again. I know what it's like to refuse to associate with fellow Christians because you're ashamed to be associated with them after watching them wound, ostracize, or harshly judge you or your loved ones. I was the wandering prodigal who turned my back on God because I couldn't separate Christ from what others called "Christianity."

While I may not have been willing to follow the God who had been modeled to me my entire childhood, I desperately wanted a God who was waiting to extend grace to me. I wanted someone who'd love *all* of me completely. That God . . . I'd consider following. No one in my life seemed to know *that* kind of Savior, but my heart was desperate to find Him.

Faith and Mental Health Care Can Coexist

After much healing and many years in therapy, I came to know Jesus and to embrace His body—the church. As an active member of my church today, I am passionate about helping bridge the gap that often exists between people who are struggling with their mental health and the Christian community. The church should be the first place we go to find healthy, restorative relationships and healing, but unfortunately, that doesn't always happen.

Due to broken bodies and a broken world, the issue of mental health isn't going away. In the United States alone, anxiety affects forty million people every year . . .

forty million. Over sixteen million Americans suffer from a depressive disorder. Nearly eight million adults suffer from Post-Traumatic Stress Disorder (PTSD).[1] And that doesn't even touch on the mental health statistics involving our kids, which have skyrocketed in the past several years, particularly following the COVID-19 pandemic.

Now imagine those suffering individuals turning toward their local church for help and instead of finding resources, support, and open arms, they only find shame, judgment, and blank stares. The truth is, friends, the church as it is today—and at times Christian culture, no matter how well-intentioned—is not always educated or equipped to deal with mental health struggles. In fact, sometimes it does more harm than good. I cannot tell you how many people have told me they no longer attend church because of the deep wounding and rejection they have experienced from other believers who perpetuate the fallacy that mental health struggles have to do with a lack of faith, personal failings, or sinful life choices.

Too often in the church, we communicate explicitly or implicitly to weary believers that there is no place for them in the body of Christ until they are "healed." We treat individuals with mental health struggles as weak links, as lesser Christians, or even as people who are walking in sin.

We have to do better. We have a chance as the church to be a hospital for the hurting, a light in the darkness, and a beacon of hope, love, and redemption for those who are struggling.

As you'll see in the following pages, and as you may have discovered in your own life, you *can* be a Christian and still struggle with your mental health and suicidal thoughts. You *can* have faith that will move mountains but still have days when you cannot move yourself out of bed. You *can* love Jesus with all your heart and still rely heavily on a therapist to walk you through life's issues and traumas. You *can* believe that God holds the entire world in His hands but still find yourself in the middle of the mother of all panic attacks because everything feels out of control.

There is a place for both faith and mental health care to coexist, and that is where transformation and recovery can be found: in Jesus *and* therapy.

I write this book as someone who has personal mental health struggles—and as someone who longs to see the church offer healing, not hurt, to those who are suffering.

If you've been hanging on by a thread to your faith, feel like an outsider in the body of Christ, or have faced rejection over your mental health, this book was written for you.

If you feel angry with God and don't know how to forgive the people who hurt you in His name, this book is for you.

If you are a parent, child, spouse, or sibling who lives with someone who wrestles with mental health issues, this book is for you.

If you are a pastor, counselor, family member, or friend seeking to understand and embrace people who live with mental health conditions, this book is for you.

In the coming chapters, we are going to do the following:

- Address common misconceptions about believers and mental health

- Discuss the church and its role in dealing with mental illness
- Work on identifying, acknowledging, and releasing past wounds
- Dismantle false beliefs about ourselves and our faith and replace them with truth
- Discuss pivotal biblical figures who wrestled with their mental health
- Build a personal and professional support system
- Examine the benefits of therapy
- Walk through practical steps to working through church hurt
- Talk about how to rebuild our spiritual foundation in the truth of Christ
- Firmly establish our identity in Jesus and our place in the church

I know firsthand that some wounds only Christ can heal, and I believe that He desires to walk with you every step of the way through your healing journey. With that in mind, at the end of each chapter, you'll find suggestions for spiritual application.

Because I personally have experienced the power of Jesus and professional therapy working together, especially for those of us who have trauma in our past or present, I also include at the end of each chapter questions, conversations, and action steps you can discuss with your therapist.

No matter where you are on your faith journey, I'd love to come alongside you and share my story and the lessons I've learned along the way as we dispel the common misconceptions about believers who suffer from mental health conditions. My hope is that by the time you turn the last page of this book, you'll see the abundant life available to you, the hope waiting despite the diagnosis, and the truth about how valuable you are to Jesus and the people around you.

Your story isn't over yet.

One

The Reason for My Wars

Identifying Abuse, Legalism, and Grace

> Violators cannot live with the truth: survivors cannot
> live without it. . . . But the truth won't go away.
> It will keep surfacing until it is recognized. Truth
> will outlast any campaigns mounted against it, no
> matter how mighty, clever, or long. It is invincible.
>
> —CHRYSTINE OKSANA, *SAFE PASSAGE TO HEALING*

Trigger Warning: This chapter discusses child abuse ranging from physical to emotional abuse, as well as spiritual abuse. Some readers may find the author's recollections of prior abuse distressing.

Every kid deserves a childhood where they can spend their most formative years experiencing innocence, belonging, love, joy, and physical and emotional safety. The kids who actually get such an experience? Well, they are the lucky ones. If your experience with the people who should have protected you wasn't a good one, you're not alone. There are many of us who still bear the wounds of a past

9

that was not our fault. Please know that you're seen and understood in this space.

I was an infant when my father's physical abuse of me began. As my mom tells it, I earned his wrath because I kept him awake, crying from colic. His anger was only matched in intensity by my mom's fear of him. So, with no one to intervene, his episodes built in intensity throughout my childhood and ranged from punching me until I blacked out to screaming that I was going to hell as he beat me with a belt. The physical abuse evolved into what I can only describe as narcissistic psychological warfare as I entered my preteen and teenage years.

I tried to please my father—oh, how I tried. As a young child, I would always color him pictures and write him notes and try to endear myself to him. As a teen, when I no longer lived with him, I was the live-action Cinderella when I'd come to visit—ironing his work clothes, making his bed, cleaning his home, and cooking for my siblings despite not being the oldest child. When you are raised in an abusive home where love is conditional or absent, you will do almost anything to feel it, even if only for a moment. Everything within me yearned to be Daddy's girl. If I'd known then what I know now, I could have saved myself a lifetime of chasing after his love and approval. But what I didn't realize was that as a narcissist, my father was incapable of providing the emotional support and nurturing I needed and deserved.

When I was only seven years old, Dad walked out on our family, leaving behind my mom, my older brother, my little sister, and me. His abandonment broke me. I still remember that sunny afternoon in Guam, when he and my mom sat me down at our round oak dining room table and told me that once we arrived at our next military duty station in Hawaii, they would be getting a divorce. I don't recall my mother saying a word during this conversation, which made it clear that Dad was driving the decision. Due to an extensive amount of trauma, many of my memories are repressed, and it is always significant to me when I retain a memory from my childhood—and this one seems as clear as if it happened yesterday.

At that time, the only thing my young heart understood was that I was the only daughter without a dad to take me to our church's father–daughter dance. I did not realize I was grieving a love I'd never had and a relationship that had never existed outside of my dreams. It didn't occur to me that his decision to leave was my only way of escaping a daily life in an ever-precarious environment and living in constant fear of his angry outbursts.

True to his word, my dad began the divorce process (and found his next wife) within months of being stationed in Hawaii. I wish I could tell you that my life improved in my father's absence, that my parents' coparenting couldn't have been better, and that both parents put my emotional well-being and physical safety first. But instead, I lived the rest of my childhood and adolescence deeply afraid of the father who'd moved only five minutes away from us with his new wife—far enough for me to feel the loss of his presence in our home, yet close enough to continue disappointing and hurting me.

When Dad and his wife decided to move from Hawaii to the mainland, I was heartbroken. I knew what it meant—he was moving on without us, without me. I'd failed to earn his unattainable love or to gain any positive attention when he was just minutes away. Once he moved thousands of miles away, I wouldn't even be able to try. I wouldn't realize it for decades, but watching my dad walk away prompted countless years of me chasing after people to love me, despite having such low self-esteem that I never once believed I was worthy of their love.

As I approached my teen years without an objective adult to help me walk through the pain of my father's abuse and abandonment, my negative self-beliefs were slowly solidifying. I couldn't shake the feeling that I was innately unworthy of saving. If I were worth protecting, wouldn't someone have jumped in front of me to take my father's hits? For years, I waited for someone to recognize the irreversible and damaging imprint this abuse caused in my life, but no one intervened. And so, I found myself growing up faster than any child should have to.

Filling My Father's Shoes

At the recommendation of the naval officer who had originally introduced my parents to each other, my family started attending a nondenominational church when we first moved to the island. When Dad moved out, we ended up moving in with the officer's family while my mom got back on her feet.

Due to Hawaii's distance from the continental United States, we were completely isolated from all family and friends. No one visited us, and we could not afford to fly back to see them, so my mom always told us the church was our family. They were all we had, and they knew it. If you look at the pattern in most cults, abusive relationships, and toxic churches, it often starts with isolation from your friends, family, and at times, the entire outside world.

Sadly, domestic childhood abuse is disturbingly common. What I didn't realize at the time was that by attending that church, we were simply replacing one type of abuse with another: spiritual abuse.

The lack of a loving paternal relationship coupled with the desperate desire for attention from my father set the stage for the men in my mom's church to slide into the roles of being my leader, my authority, my mentor, my big brother, and even my father figure. The implication was plainly stated: they would fill my dad's shoes. At the time, this seemed like a kind, sacrificial, loving gesture, but it ultimately ended up becoming my worst nightmare. Abe was one of those men.

When I first met Abe at church, I found him to be friendly and outgoing. He was a young newlywed, about fifteen years older than me, who had recently moved to Hawaii with his bride. Abe's bubbly wife reminded me of a cheerleader. At the ripe old age of eight, I knew very few people who were *that* enthusiastic about life, so I was naturally drawn to her. Abe and his new bride were attending the university together, and my mom would bring me to their living quarters on campus to visit with them and have reading/speech lessons with Abe, an aspiring teacher. I spoke with a lisp at the time, so my mom thought reading aloud with someone would help correct my speech patterns.

Abe told me that he was like a big brother to me. Outside of my *actual* older brother, I was missing male role models in my life, so I relished the idea of a man wanting to invest his time and attention in me. It made me believe for a minute that, just maybe, I was worthy of love.

The third male role model in my life outside of my father and Abe was an elder in our church, Brent. He spoke loudly, with self-imposed authority, ensuring everyone noticed him and his position. According to Brent, he had the gifts of prophecy and interpretation. He was always in the front row at church, ready to share the words the

Lord had just given him, half of which were terrifying to me as a kid.

In our church, we had something called "home fellowships"—weekly small groups that met in someone's home. In a typical church, these meetings might have included worship, a Bible study, or a discussion expounding on the Sunday sermon topic. Instead, the group that met in our home, which was led by Brent, turned into the Brent Show—a toxic dumping ground for him to speak his mind and flex his authority, without an ounce of accountability.

Initially, hosting the home fellowship at our house made me feel quite special because I'd help Mom clean and set up all the drinks and refreshments. I'd been told by my church leaders that I had the gift of hospitality, and I held on to that rare piece of praise with a death grip. In retrospect, I now understand the patriarchal views that shaped that praise. Heavily influenced by the teachings of Bill Gothard, the patriarchal founder of the Institute in Basic Life Principles, my male church leadership thought women were only good for cleaning, serving, raising babies, and cooking. Gothard's organization was recently the subject of the Amazon documentary *Shiny Happy People*, which gave the world greater insight into this disturbing organization.

Controlled by the Church

No one who attended our church back then was interested in just being a stereotypical "Sunday Christian." If that were the type of Christian you wanted to be, one who could simply pop in for the service and then go about your business the rest of the week, odds were you'd run for the hills after attending our hyper-controlling congregation or, better yet, be excommunicated! It was an early Sunday prayer, Sunday service, Sunday night home fellowship, Wednesday night service, church game nights, and camping trips kind of situation. If you thought you could just show your face on Sunday morning and then act however you wanted on Monday, you'd be in for a rude awakening. Church leaders kept tabs on members at all times. My best friend was the pastor's daughter, and her life was even more of a fishbowl than mine.

This intense level of involvement was expected from all church members, resulting in a hyper-dependence on the church leadership. Even adults seemed incapable of making decisions for themselves. The leadership had their nose in every family's business, freely giving opinions, advice, and criticism. It was as cultlike as you could get, and because our family was so deeply entrenched, we were highly vulnerable.

The church offered me and my siblings—who were homeschooled—our only social exposure and our only friends, as it was the only place where we spent a significant amount of time. Our experience was the epitome of the adage "It takes a village to raise a child," except the village was composed of self-righteous men whose only expectation of anyone was *nothing less than perfection.*

Though I was able to identify the abuse at the hands of my father for what it was early on, it took me well into my twenties *and* thirties to recognize the extent of spiritual abuse that occurred in my childhood church. For that reason, and because so many of us suffer with our mental health due to spiritual abuse, I want to briefly address some of the ways you can spot spiritual abuse. I believe we must identify what is not healthy and not of God before we can move further on in our healing journey. Whether or not it is obvious to you that you experienced spiritual abuse, it can be helpful to name these things, understand how abuse plays out, and reflect on if it may have happened to you.

Spiritually abusive leaders may:

- Use scripture to induce guilt, shame, or fear
- Continually tell you that you are unworthy
- Limit access to other biblical teachings and accuse leaders other than themselves of being false teachers
- Control what people listen to, read, or watch
- Make you feel guilty for questioning their authority
- Use their own outward spirituality to justify abusive behavior
- Refuse to acknowledge their own shortcomings
- Twist scripture to coerce or control people
- Claim they have closer access to God than others
- Declare that if you disobey them, you are disobeying the Lord
- Force accountability by coercing "confessions" and using inappropriate means to find out details about your life and "sins"
- Create an environment where it is unacceptable to voice disagreement or ask questions
- Overstep boundaries related to personal issues such as marriage, children, and finances

My church checked the box on every single one of these warning signs. I wish I could have known back then that the completely unattainable, legalistic existence the "church" attempted to force me to maintain was not what God required of me. If only I had understood that behind closed doors, not a single one of them was the person they portrayed themselves to be and that they were holding me to a standard that they themselves could not meet.

By Grace I Have Been Saved?

While I never experienced grace in action in that little church, it certainly impressed upon me how despicable it was to abuse it! The only option set before me was absolute perfection, so as not to risk falling into the category of "sinner."

I longed to experience the freedom of what a life under grace felt like, except grace was more of an abstract idea in this congregation rather than something you practiced giving or receiving on a regular basis. Instead, I was left to put together the only picture of Jesus I could, which was shaped by people further from His heart and character than you can imagine.

My home life had taught me that I wasn't worth loving as I was. The church reinforced that message.

My home life demonstrated that I had to earn my good standing. The church taught me that I had to earn my place with Jesus *and* that anything I earned was revocable. I always felt that my salvation was entirely dependent on how I behaved and that I was barely hanging on to it.

My home life instilled in me the belief that I'd never be good enough. My church family wholly agreed.

Every wounding message I received from being raised in a dysfunctional home was like a dagger to my heart. When the church reinforced those lies, it merely drove the pain deeper and cemented my beliefs about myself and my worth.

Within the walls of that church, I learned that God was someone to fear, a harsh taskmaster who expected my absolute obedience. And according to the church, that obedience meant 100 percent submission to *any* man who claimed to be speaking for God and serving Him. I was not to question their authority. *Obedience was to be immediate and complete.*

As I grew into adolescence in this legalistic existence, it seemed as if the list of what I could not do was continually growing:

I was not allowed to speak in church.
I was a woman; we did not do that.

I was not allowed to like boys.
They would distract me from Jesus.

I was not allowed to date.
We kissed dating goodbye.

I was not allowed to give forward-facing hugs to any member of the opposite sex.
They could not handle the temptation of feeling my body up against theirs.

I was not allowed to watch any movies that said a single swear word or took the Lord's name in vain.
I should not be entertained by sin.

I was not allowed to listen to any secular music.
Drums and electric guitars were of the devil, and there was no such thing as Christian rock music.

I was not allowed to listen to any music or watch any TV at all during mandated church-wide fasts or those imposed by my mom.
I should be willing to give up everything for Jesus.

I was not allowed to be friends with the pastor's daughter anymore.

Even she was a bad influence on me. She talked to me about boys, wrote me notes during the sermon—you know, the usual "deadly" sins!

I could not appropriately identify and label the intense legalism of my childhood church or my upbringing, because it was all that I knew. Follow the rules. Be a flawless Christian. Mistakes are not allowed.

While I passionately followed Christ in my younger years and desired to be like Him more than anything, the absence of grace would eventually drive a wedge between me and my Savior, severely affecting my mental health and sending me into a long, dark period of depression.

God's Honest Truth

Perhaps one or many parts of my church experience resonate with you. If so, I am so sorry that you have to unlearn those "core" beliefs you now realize are unbiblical. Though at times I'm sure it must feel as if you are alone on this journey, I promise: you are not. Many of us have been where you are now and are still fighting through it. I talk to people on a regular basis who are doing the hard and holy work of processing their church experience and beginning to flush out all the lies that were passed off to them as God's truth.

If you're curious to hear what God says about grace, you probably need to hear as badly as I did that there is *nothing* you can do to earn God's love. His love existed before the world began, and it is already yours—there is nothing you can do to lose it. No mistake or sin could ever separate you from the immense love God has for you

(Romans 8:38-39). In fact, the Bible is full of verses that demonstrate why being perfect is *not* what God requires of His children:

> Then they said to him, "What must we do, to be
> doing the works of God?" Jesus answered them,
> "This is the work of God, that you believe in him
> whom he has sent."
>   (John 6:38-39)

> So we are made right with God through faith and
> not by obeying the law.
>   (Romans 3:28 NLT)

> "I do not set aside the grace of God, for if
> righteousness could be gained through the law,
> Christ died for nothing!"
>   (Galatians 2:21 NIV)

> God saved you by his grace when you believed. And
> you can't take credit for this; it is a gift from God.
> Salvation is not a reward for the good things we
> have done, so none of us can boast about it.
>   (Ephesians 2:8-9 NLT)

> For Christ has already accomplished the purpose for
> which the law was given. As a result, all who believe
> in him are made right with God.
>   (Romans 10:4 NLT)

I don't know about you, but I didn't grow up hearing about *these* verses from the Bible, which is odd, because I was forced to read and memorize my Bible without ceasing! Isn't it comforting to know that the love, the belonging, and the acceptance we have been searching for our whole lives are right here, waiting for us? It certainly didn't feel like those things were extended to us when the church was rejecting us, did it? I had to walk through countless years of pain, rejection, abuse, and judgment before I could move on from the gaping wounds my church left behind.

As you work to carve out your own path—or to help someone else carve out theirs—through the feelings and negative beliefs that have been planted in your mind and soul, you will begin the work of breaking down the walls of "religion." Through this challenging but freeing process, you'll gain a deeper and healthier understanding of how God feels about you—and about all of us. Church was never meant to be this way.

Jesus and Therapy

Jesus

Maybe you haven't been on speaking terms with God for a while and you don't even know how to begin to pray. If this is your reality, put on "Kind" by Cory Asbury or "Crazy About You" by Tauren Wells and take a moment to just sit. As you listen, consider that the angry and unapproachable image you might have of Jesus isn't a reflection of the One who welcomes you to come and lay down your heavy load at His feet. Even if nothing else makes sense right now, know that His heart for you is *kind*.

Therapy

If you have a history of childhood abuse or trauma—including spiritual abuse—it might be beneficial to ask your therapist to help you recognize ways your earthly caregivers shaped your view of who God is and how He feels about you. If this is the first time you're realizing you were subjected to spiritual abuse, work with your counselor to identify which aspects of spiritually abusive leaders, as identified in this chapter, are consistent with your experiences.

Two

Hard to Love

Becoming Mindful of Inaccurate Core Self and Spiritual Beliefs

I have loved you with an everlasting love;
Therefore with lovingkindness I have drawn you
and continued My faithfulness to you.

—JEREMIAH 31:3 (AMP)

Trigger Warning: This chapter discusses the topics of child abuse and the spiritual abuse of women.

I was fifteen years old, sitting in a room full of my closest friends and family at our weekly home fellowship group, and we'd just finished watching the newest *Veggie Tales*. (You know you're a church kid when that's the only acceptable form of entertainment!) Brent and other church members began praying over my brother, sister, and me because we were about to fly to the Midwest to spend time with our father. They prayed for protection as we traveled, for my siblings and I to be a light and a witness to our father and his girlfriend, and for God to keep our faith strong in the face of opposition.

This particular Sunday night, Brent had something special he wanted to say to me in the presence of the entire group. He began, "You've gone too far, Tabitha. Even God cannot reach you and if He could, He probably wouldn't want to. You're beyond saving. You're like a stubborn donkey." (Almost every man in my church had called me this at some point. It was their religiously "acceptable" way of calling me a you-know-what.) "I'm just going to stop trying to help you from this point on. I wash my hands of you."

This man had known me since I was a little girl. I trusted him. I'd bought into every "prophecy" he'd ever spoken over me. I thought God had surrounded me with godly men to fill the hole my father's absence had left in my life. And I believed these men were free to treat me however they wanted to "in the name of the Lord."

In the wake of Brent's words, I sat stunned, crushed, and trying to process that I had just been publicly disowned and rejected not just by a significant figure in our church, but by Jesus *Himself*! Was I really beyond reaching and not worth saving? As I sat in the ensuing silence, not one person in that room cut Brent off, argued with him, or stood up for me. In a group full of close friends, parents, and siblings, not a word was uttered in my defense. To this day, I often wonder if that moment would have had less of a detrimental impact and how my life might have gone differently had anyone intervened on my behalf.

If you're wondering what prompted Brent's outburst, I wasn't a bad kid. But after experiencing so much abuse, I'd changed. How could I not have? Brent and the other church leaders had watched me gradually become emotionally defeated, shut down, disillusioned, and depressed. Yet instead of showing me compassion or offering help, they interpreted my brokenness as disobedience. I didn't let anyone in; therefore, I must be difficult and stubborn. My primal desire to protect myself, when no one else was doing so, was viewed as an act of rebellion and a sign of a heart not submitted to my spiritual leaders and parents.

Betrayal by the Brethren

To add insult to extensive injury, within that same year, a visiting "prophet" spent a couple of weeks at our church. Apparently, he had been "sent" to confirm what Brent had spoken over me. All he had to do was blow into town, claim the gift of prophecy, and then—*bam!* He was given the freedom to speak "words from the Lord" over vulnerable men, women, and children. Not a single member of our congregation knew who this individual was, where he had come from, or how he'd found our church. All I knew at the time was that I found it odd that a "prophet" from Heaven chain-smoked cigarettes and dressed like he'd just gotten pulled out of a luau to deliver his messages from above.

So there I sat in Brent's home for our home fellowship meeting (we alternated meeting in different church members' homes) when this visiting pseudo-prophet asked me to come sit in the chair in the middle of the room so he could speak over me. This was a very Pentecostal thing to do, and my church was all about the "laying on of hands" and speaking prophetic words over church members. In fact, they would record it on tape anytime you were "prophesied" over, and to this day I still have a cassette tape from the church with some of my "words from the Lord" on it. Every red flag you can imagine was going off in my head about this guy, but it appeared I was the only person suspicious of his heavenly citizenship. At that age, I didn't know I could say no to a church leader or that I could tell my mom how uncomfortable this man was making me and escape the situation. Plus, if I refused to accept prayer, I could only *imagine* what worse things would be thought of me. What kind of Christian would that make me? Resigned, I sat and surrendered myself to whatever was about to happen.

Loudly and with great authority in his voice, the "prophet" began to speak his "word from the Lord": "God sees your rebellion. He will punish you for your attitude. You will go to your grave early for your rebellious heart and ways."

Wait . . . what? I looked around incredulously at the rest of my church family, who were laying hands on me like this dude was speaking a blessing over me rather than condemning me to an early grave. They had their eyes closed as if this were some sacred moment. People I loved were even nodding along. Feeling like I had no other choice, I sat there unmoving.

I wasn't old enough to drive and get away from there, and I didn't know where I would go anyway. The only people I knew were church members, and I wouldn't be safe in any of their homes either. Peeking through my half-closed eyelids, I waited in vain for someone to come to my defense. Instead, I sat surrounded by Christians with their arms outstretched toward me, joining in with a total stranger as he spoke words of death and destruction over my young life.

The betrayal I felt at that moment was all-consuming. The fact that not a single person in that room felt a protective impulse toward me *still* disappoints me to this day. This lack of protection was precisely why I didn't trust any of the adults in my life at the time. And this was just one of many situations—all of which I'd eventually spend countless years unpacking in therapy—that would continue to be allowed and encouraged.

Into the Lion's Den

As the months went on, my depression deepened. I could feel it pulling me further and further under with each passing day. Besides the spiritual abuse I was suffering at church, I was also experiencing a hopeless toxic cycle of narcissistic abuse from my father, and though I wanted to, I could not run away from my forced annual visits. I felt my desperation growing as I approached my sixteenth birthday. Wasn't I at the age where I should have a choice whether I spent time with my dad? If so, why was time with him being forced on me? My mental health hanging on by a thin, rapidly fraying thread, I went into that summer's visitation with my dad feeling like I was drowning. The leaders in my church had washed their hands of me, and now I was about to walk into the lion's den.

Even in my earliest years, I understood my dad didn't truly love me. I knew if I wanted to be treated decently and not trigger his temper, I had to walk a delicate tightrope with both my words and my behavior. I was painfully aware that a "good relationship" with my dad was entirely dependent on me "acting right." As you can probably guess, this tumultuous balancing act with my earthly father didn't stop with my dad. By the time I was a teenager, it had come to represent how I viewed my relationship with my heavenly Father as well.

I remember the precise moment my father spoke aloud the words I'd always feared to be true. I was sitting on my brother's bed and Dad was casually playing solitaire on the '90s desktop computer a few feet away from me when he flippantly uttered the words that pierced my heart:

"If your mom and I would have known how things were going to work out, we wouldn't have had kids."

At his words, I started choking back sobs. The magnitude of his statement hit me like a freight train: my own dad wished I'd never been born. The thing is, you can think you know how someone feels about you, but there is a death that happens when the words are spoken aloud. There's no more pretense to hide behind.

Instead of comforting me, my dad began belittling me over my audacity to cry, until my older brother came in and said, "OK, Dad, just stop. Look at her. Obviously, she's had enough." Despite him also being conditioned to tolerate my father's outbursts, something in my brother recognized I'd hit my breaking point.

I waited to phone my mom until my father was at work the next day, so he wouldn't hear my conversation. Curling up in Dad's favorite recliner where he'd sit at the end of his workday and have me take off his shoes for him, I called my mother, crying. I begged to be allowed to change my ticket and just come home. "Well, you know how he'll react if you do that," she said. "It will probably be the end of your relationship. You don't want to burn that bridge because somewhere down the road, you might want to try again with him."

There it sat, the entire future of our relationship in the hands of a tragically unstable teenager. But how could I stay? Being near my dad was destroying me—there was no escaping his abuse when we were under the same roof. My mind was going to a very dark place, and I could feel my mental health collapsing under the weight brought on by the full realization that I was unwanted, unloved, and supposedly destined for a tragically early death. It was like watching a slow-motion train wreck I was powerless to stop.

I ended up staying the whole summer. Ultimately, the guilt over not wanting to be the one responsible for the permanent demise of the relationship with my dad proved to be stronger than my instinct for self-preservation.

I had no way of knowing it then, but my choice to stay for the remainder of the summer would change the course of my young life. In a desperate effort to numb the pain, I started stealing Dad's alcohol, experimenting with smoking, and playing with fire, both figuratively and literally. Something in me had shifted. It felt as though my internal dialogue had been solidified. My fate to die young was etched in stone. Nothing mattered anymore. Perhaps it was the words that had been spoken over me that I was fundamentally unworthy and unwanted by both Jesus and my father that had me self-destructing. Regardless of the catalyst, my actions started to reflect what I now actually believed: I was a lost cause.

Unworthy of Love

Because I experienced rejection from numerous foundational people in my life early on, I spent my most formative years attempting to earn love from those around me. When those I turned to failed to offer me either love or protection, I would think, *If they refuse to love or accept me or be a part of my life . . . why would* anyone else *love me, accept me, or stay?* Unsurprisingly, this viewpoint was projected onto God as well. After all, I was damaged goods, irreversibly messed up, and too hard for anyone—even my heavenly Father—to love.

Since rejection from fellow Christians had permeated much of my young life, that experience conditioned me to spend my teens and twenties expecting the rejection I believed I deserved in every subsequent relationship. How could I trust the best about people or God when all I'd experienced was the worst of humanity?

If you find yourself in a place where your worth has been defined by the misconceptions and wounding messages of others, my hope is to help you unravel the lies that have been packaged and presented to you as God's perspective. But before we deep dive into God's character and how He feels about you—which we'll do in the coming chapters—let's first take a moment to identify some foundational falsehoods. Recognizing these false beliefs is imperative to our healing journeys, because what we think to be true about ourselves often becomes our internal dialogue. And when that internal dialogue dictates how we feel we deserve to be treated, it can keep us from pursuing or accepting all the goodness God has for us.

No matter how many lies we've come to believe throughout our lives, there's still hope. As we evaluate the areas where we haven't valued ourselves in the same way that Jesus does, we have the power to shift our perspective and change our narrative through healing, counseling, and prayer.

To receive God's truth about what defines us, the lie that we're inherently undesirable or unlovable must be dismantled. Identifying those areas where our circumstances, rather than God, have dictated our worth will be key to our healing journey. As we slowly begin to heal and recognize our own value, some important things will happen:

- Unhealthy habits and negative mindsets, like categorizing ourselves as a waste of time and space, will shift and evolve into healthy self-love.
- We will no longer perceive our basic needs for love, protection, and belonging as an inconvenience to others.

- We will finally be free to receive the words of truth that God speaks over us, as we release every lie, condemnation, and judgment that has been spoken over our lives.

As you read over the reminders below of who Jesus says you are, feel free to write down any core beliefs about yourself that don't reflect the Father's heart of God—which are false beliefs that you will want to work on releasing. We are each invited to root ourselves in a new identity that is found in Jesus alone.

Identity in Christ Affirmations

I am a child of the King.
But you are God's chosen treasure—priests who are kings, a spiritual "nation" set apart as God's devoted ones. He called you out of darkness to experience his marvelous light, and now he claims you as his very own.
(1 Peter 2:9 TPT)

I am valuable.
For you know that God paid a ransom to save you from the empty life you inherited from your ancestors. And it was not paid with mere gold or silver, which lose their value. It was the precious blood of Christ, the sinless, spotless Lamb of God.
(1 Peter 1:18-19 NLT)

I am chosen.
Even before he made the world, God loved us and chose us in Christ to be holy and without fault in his eyes.
(Ephesians 1:4 NLT)

I am heard.

I am passionately in love with God because
    he listens to me.
He hears my prayers and answers them.
As long as I live I'll keep praying to him,
for he stoops down to listen to my heart's cry.
    (Psalm 116:1-2 TPT)

I am enough.

Everything we could ever need for life and godliness
has already been deposited in us by his divine
power. For all this was lavished upon us through the
rich experience of knowing him who has called us
by name and invited us to come to him through a
glorious manifestation of his goodness.
    (2 Peter 1:3 TPT)

I am not alone.

The LORD himself goes before you and will be with
you; he will never leave you nor forsake you.
    (Deuteronomy 31:8 NIV)

I am accepted.

You will bring God glory when you accept and
welcome one another as partners, just as the
Anointed One has fully accepted you and received
you as his partner.
    (Romans 15:7 TPT)

I am blameless.

. . . just as [in His love] He chose us in Christ [actually
selected us for Himself as His own] before the
foundation of the world, so that we would be holy

[that is, consecrated, set apart for Him, purpose-
driven] and blameless in His sight.
(Ephesians 1:4 AMP)

I am loved.
So now I live with the confidence that there is nothing
in the universe with the power to separate us from
God's love. I'm convinced that his love will triumph
over death, life's troubles, fallen angels, or dark rulers
in the heavens. There is nothing in our present or
future circumstances that can weaken his love.
(Romans 8:38 TPT)

I am God's masterpiece.
For we are God's masterpiece. He has created us
anew in Christ Jesus, so we can do the good things
he planned for us long ago.
(Ephesians 2:10 NLT)

Jesus and Therapy

Jesus

Will you invite Jesus into your healing journey going forward? Ask Him for His strength as you begin to peel back layers of deep-rooted beliefs, and ask Him to reveal the Father's heart toward you and the good plans that are in store for your future.

Therapy

Discuss with your therapist your desire to be more mindful of negative or untrue self-talk. Allow that professional to walk you through the process of identifying those core self and spiritual beliefs that you're beginning to recognize are inaccurate.

Three

You Don't Look Like Jesus

Navigating Condemnation over Mental Health

> These people show respect to Me with their mouth,
> and honor Me with their lips, but their heart is far
> from Me. Their worship of Me is worth nothing.
> They teach rules that men have made.
>
> —ISAIAH 29:13 (NLV)

Trigger Warning: This chapter discusses suicide and spiritual abuse.

After being demoted to second-class citizen by a congregation I dreaded returning to, and being deeply wounded by my father, I came home that summer as a sixteen-year-old who was more broken than ever. I didn't know how much longer I could contain my pain. My views about myself, God, and the church were becoming more and more tainted.

Unfortunately for me, the church I grew up in had two unspoken codes of conduct: First, you had better put on a happy face. It didn't matter if your only child had been taken by cancer, if you were going through a horrific divorce, if you were enduring abuse, or if you were contemplating suicide—you better count it all joy and turn that frown upside down, Sister! Second, if someone asked how you were doing, the appropriate response was, "Fine." It didn't matter if tears were streaming down your face; you were always *fine*. No one wanted to hear anything different. Authenticity wasn't welcome, only toxic positive Christianity.

Despite knowing that silent suffering (while counting it all joy, of course) was expected of me, I couldn't continue to stay quiet. I had to try to talk to someone. I needed someone to know how much I was hurting, how lost I felt, and how scared I was of this darkness swallowing me whole. I ached for a safe and protective adult who'd pull me up from the pit I had fallen into. Surely, someone felt I was worthy of saving.

As I searched for someone I could trust with my story, my church was going through a huge upheaval. The senior pastor's family had suddenly left the church because of a family emergency, and so our much younger, inexperienced associate pastor, Abe, took over faster than you could blink. Yes, this was the same young man I'd met when he was a university student. Suddenly, someone who'd been in a brotherly role in my life was my "spiritual authority," and boy, did he make sure I knew it.

To complicate matters further, Abe was also the principal of the Christian school operated by our church. I had started working there as a teacher's aide when I was fifteen years old, so Abe was already heavily involved in my daily life. Being my pastor and my boss turned out to be a lethal combination of power.

Fire and Brimstone

When I finally worked up the nerve to tell my church leaders about the deep depression I was experiencing, I didn't leave any cards on the table. I needed Abe and the others to know that I was ready to end my life just to escape it all. I don't know what I expected to hear in response to my costly confession, but it wasn't the flippant words that met my ears. "Well, you'll go to Hell if you commit suicide," they told me.

My heart longed to hear that I was loved, that no one wanted to lose me, that I was not a bad seed, that my future was bright, and that just maybe life would get better. Deep inside, I wanted some type of affirmation: that my life had a purpose and it would be a mistake to cut it short before I could experience all that God had for me.

Feeling as though Abe had just slapped me in the face, I could only respond with, "Well, I'm already *in* hell every day of my life, so I'll just trade one hell for the other." Everything was so dark, so painful, so hopeless, it didn't matter much to me by that point where I would spend eternity. I wasn't sure I believed in an afterlife anyway. All that mattered was being anywhere but trapped in my present life.

My brash young pastor had not yet experienced counseling a church member through anything, had no knowledge of mental health conditions, and was very open about the fact that he hadn't lived a life where he'd experienced any hardship. On top of that, I was his first guinea pig for experimenting with counseling. Rather than referring me to a professional counselor, or at least throwing out an "I'll pray for you," he continually said things that made my situation feel dramatically worse. He repeatedly spewed his flawed theology at me:

"Suicide victims aren't allowed into Heaven."

"God can't forgive you if you hurt yourself."

"You wouldn't be in this position with your mental health to begin with if your faith were stronger."

"Do you really need antidepressants, or do you just need to trust God more?"

All this spiritual abuse was coming from a man who'd known me since I was seven years old. I babysat his daughter. He called himself my big brother. I genuinely believed he cared about me, yet his portrayal of God's heart toward me was false and harmful. He had no idea that his astounding lack of compassion, understanding, godly wisdom, and just flat-out common sense was doing far more harm than good.

The mistreatment didn't stop with Abe, Brent, and other male leadership in the church. Almost every interaction I had with other believers regarding my depression deepened my feelings of alienation, strengthened my resolve to not trust them with my pain, and gave me a very early understanding of how much the church as a whole was lacking mental health awareness and the resources to handle mental health issues appropriately.

Because the harshest, most judgmental group of individuals I encountered on my journey through mental health challenges were always Christians, I deeply struggled as a young person attempting to defend myself against false accusations and judgments from the people I was supposed to be looking to for an example.

If, like me, you're living with any long-term mental or physical illness, you've probably encountered several types of stereotypical reactions after a fellow believer discovered that you, God forbid, wrestle with your emotional well-being. For my sanity, I've had to begin labeling these stereotypical reactions, so I can recognize them for what they are—which, by the way, is far from the heart of God toward me. Perhaps you, too, have experienced some of these individuals in your own journey. Let's take a look at some of these judgmental "characters" that I—and quite possibly you, too—have found in the church.

The Holier-Than-Thou Pharisee

This individual cannot possibly relate to your struggles, because they are too occupied with pretending they don't have any struggles of their own. They are too blessed to be stressed. (Man, I hate that phrase!) They are convinced that *you* are the one who's doing something wrong; otherwise, God would be blessing you. The pedestal they put themselves on prevents them from offering any true wisdom, authenticity, or compassion. They are so far out of touch with the heart of God, yet they continually speak in His name, convinced that they are His appointed mouthpiece. There is a humility that can only grow when you're less focused on judging people for their dirty feet and battered, road-worn sandals and more focused on getting on your knees, rolling up your sleeves, and washing feet as Jesus modeled. Let's just say that the Holier-Than-Thou Pharisees don't have that humility.

The Too-Heavenly-Minded-for-Earthly-Good Christian

We all know at least one of these people. Their every response is that they will pray for you, but they seem incapable of offering any tangible assistance. Your physical or mental health diagnosis can just be surrendered to the

Lord, as far as they're concerned. They don't understand the psychology behind why you are having a panic attack; why your PTSD is triggered by certain sights, sounds, or situations; or why you can't get out of bed when chronic pain rears its ugly head. They have a scripture for everything but don't make the time or offer the resources to help meet your immediate needs, whether that's giving you a ride to the doctor, picking up your groceries, or babysitting your kids while you go to counseling.

It's great to have your mind set on eternity, but not to the extent that you lose sight of God's will for you to be His hands and feet to people who are hurting and lost in *this* life.

The Ill-Equipped Church Leader

Imagine going to your pastor or elder for help, feeling like you're at the end of your rope and desperate for some hope and encouragement, only to be told that you've brought this on yourself—that you've displeased God or done something to warrant this "punishment." Perhaps they discount your significant trauma or sweep abuse under the rug. You walk out of their office feeling more alone and defeated than ever.

Yes, there are some pastors and church leaders who are quite good at counseling people through trauma, pain, addictions, and mental health struggles, thanks to previous training or a perspective gained through personal experience. However, seminary does not provide a degree in psychology, and a good pastor will recognize where their expertise ends and refer you to the appropriate source to get help.

I passionately believe we need mental health awareness and sensitivity training for church leaders. Additionally, as the church, we need immediate resources on hand so we can refer individuals for counseling, rehab, and other forms of help.

False Condemnation

When it comes to living with a mental health struggle, we can draw many parallels between the Bible's account of Job and his friends and modern-day interactions. At first, the Bible tell us, when Job's friends heard of all the loss and suffering he was going through, they set out to sympathize with him and comfort him. Seeing the tremendous pain their friend was in, three of Job's friends sat in silence with him for seven days and nights.

So far, so good, right? By all accounts, the visiting gentlemen were well-meaning. They had come to comfort. They sat and empathized with this man, so wracked with grief and pain that they hardly recognized him.

I think this is sometimes how things begin with certain friends or family who have good intentions. They start out seeking to comfort you, feeling sympathetic toward your mental health struggles. They may even be helpful initially and respond appropriately when a crisis arises. However, as time passes and your pain does not quickly subside, they begin to do what Job's friends did: give in to the human urge to find the source of your suffering. They begin to assign blame and attempt to problem-solve for you and oversimplify things:

"If you would just pray more, heavenly help would come."

"If you memorize enough scriptures, you can make the suicidal thoughts go away."

"If you were strong enough, you could train your mind not to think this way."

"You just need to command your soul to bless
the Lord."

"This too shall pass."

"Count it all joy."

And, perhaps my all-time favorite, which is sprinkled
over every hard, uncomfortable situation:

"God never gives you more than you can handle."

If you try throwing out that last "helpful" cookie-cutter
response to someone in the depths of depression, I can
pretty much guarantee they're not thinking, *Thank you so
much for reminding me of God's holy truth!* Instead, they're
making a mental note never to be vulnerable with you again.

Rather than bringing hope and life to our plight,
well-intentioned platitudes offer little but condemnation
and shame. And being falsely condemned is certainly
something Job would know a thing or two about.

Exhibit A: Job opened his mouth to speak.

Cursing the day he was born, Job finally gave voice to
his pain and despair. He despised his life, and he wasn't
even trying to hide it. I imagine most reasonable people,
hearing all that Job had lost and suffered through, would
have given Job a bit of grace at this moment . . . but not his
friends. Upon hearing Job's outburst, Job's friend Eliphaz
inserted himself into the conversation. After a humble brag
about himself, reminding Job of all the people he'd helped
and the wisdom he'd spoken into others' lives, Eliphaz
started slipping in accusations and suggestions that God
was punishing Job. Perhaps Job brought all these trials
on himself, and they were merely the product of God's
discipline:

"Remember now, who ever perished being innocent?
Or where were the upright destroyed?
According to what I have seen,
those who plow wrongdoing
and those who sow trouble harvest it."
(Job 4:7-8 NASB)

"Behold, happy is the person whom God disciplines,
So do not reject the discipline of the Almighty.
For He inflicts pain, and gives relief;
He wounds, but His hands also heal."
(Job 5:17-18 NASB)

After Eliphaz basically suggested that Job's pain and loss were of his own doing, Job finally declared to his friends,

"Oh that you would be completely silent!"
(Job 13:5 NASB)

Often, people's negative or hurtful reactions toward those struggling with mental health conditions are rooted purely in ignorance. Having no idea where the other person is coming from or the degree to which they're struggling, they offer what they feel are practical solutions for what they perceive to be the problem. In their mind, they're helping—their friend needs assistance, so they are coming to the rescue. Unfortunately for the recipient of the advice, the well-meaning friend often has no comprehension of the complexities surrounding mental illness or the potential trauma behind it. And if the unsolicited advice continues, it often leads to the demise of the relationship.

Just Sit with Me

Job had gone through unspeakable loss and was understandably consumed by anguish. His words didn't just go on for what would become one short chapter. Oh, no, he let it all out. In fact, not until the thirty-eighth chapter of the book of Job did Job's dialogue with his friends end—as God began addressing him. Job needed to be heard. He needed to grieve out loud. He needed to recount the trauma that he was still very much in the midst of by the time God responded to his cries.

There were two women in my childhood and teenage years who grew to mean so much to me because they would do just that. Before I was able to attend therapy regularly, they would simply sit and listen to me tell the tales of the same trauma as many times as I needed to. I have no doubt these women saved my life on multiple occasions by just sitting with me in my pain.

When a person is suffering from depression, they often just need a safe space—with safe people—where they can share their feelings. They need an outlet to discuss the journey that's brought them to this point in their lives. It's not a pretty process. Rarely is it even a brief conversation.

Sometimes we just need to mourn—we need someone to sit in the dark with us and hold our hand. On other days, we may need a prayer warrior to stand in the gap and go to Heaven on our behalf. A humble heart, a listening ear, and a compassionate spirit will go far in making you a safe space for someone to share their troubles with. The only way to discern whether a struggling individual needs a silent presence or tangible help is to keep showing up, be present in their suffering, and look for ways to assist.

Also, it's important to note that when it comes to mental health struggles, being made to feel like our suffering is a burden is the last thing that is needed or beneficial. When we're wrestling with God, we don't need someone to defend His character as we walk through our doubt, grief, or anger. It's a journey we must go on to build authentic faith. And God is big enough to handle our emotions and our questions.

Like Job's friends eventually learned, we must meet people where they're at. There is a season for everything under the sun, and sometimes that is a season of simply sitting in silence and weeping with those who mourn.

Second-Class Christian

An important part of meeting people where they're at is treating them, their season, and their struggles with respect. Being treated as less than, or as a second-class member of society and a "permanently broken" member of the church, is far too common. I once took a poll among friends about what they wished they could tell people about their mental health struggles. Unfortunately, as you can see by their responses, a common theme emerged of feeling judged and deemed inferior by their fellow Christians:

> "I'm not choosing to be this way."

> "I'm not lazy. I'm not refusing to try. It's not about willpower."

> "Depression and anxiety can make me sick, and at times they come with debilitating physical effects, but that doesn't mean I'm irresponsible."

> "I deserve to be treated with honor and dignity, as someone cherished by their Creator. Please don't make me feel less than."

"Every human being has brokenness, whether in their brain or their body. So please don't judge me."

"Struggling with my mental health doesn't mean I'm crazy."

"I wish the church would stop telling me my faith isn't strong enough."

"I'm not a mistake."

"I can love Jesus and have faith but still have a chemical imbalance that causes me to need an antidepressant."

God's "Ranking System"

Like my friends, my struggles left me feeling "less than," as if my value as a person and as a Christian had been weighed and measured and I'd come up short. Can you imagine if God had a ranking system of how "good" of a believer you were—a system determined by your societal, physical, or mental limitations? What if He disqualified you from being an effective member of the body of Christ simply because your body or brain worked a bit differently than the person standing next to you?

Thankfully, we don't have to imagine this reality in Heaven because Jesus doesn't rank believers with mental health struggles; He doesn't consider them second-class Christians. You aren't denied access to His throne because you wrestle with emotional afflictions. You don't mean less to Him because you face darker moments than others do. Your prayers don't get demoted because you've got a psychiatrist or a therapist on speed dial.

If the church withheld its open arms and alienated anyone suffering from a *physical* ailment or a long-term illness, it's not difficult to imagine the uproar that would follow. Instead, as they should, Christian culture celebrates those individuals for pushing forward, despite their chronic struggles or limitations. Those of us who deal with mental health conditions should not be treated any differently!

Why are we not applauding these struggling members of the body of Christ for getting up that morning and choosing to come to church, despite knowing that they may feel alienated or misunderstood? After all, some days it takes just as much strength and courage for someone battling depression or anxiety to get out of bed and face the world as someone battling a long-term illness— *because that is exactly what they are doing.* Those with mental health conditions are battling long-term, and in some cases debilitating, disorders that just happen to be invisible to the rest of the world.

Sadly, many of us *have* experienced discrimination within the walls of the church for conditions out of our control. We have been made to feel like we are not mature believers, that we are living in sin, or that we are not putting our hope in Jesus simply because of our mental health challenges.

If this is your story, you aren't alone. It breaks my heart that other believers turned you away when Christ was waiting to welcome you with open arms. I'm sorry if instead of being known by your character and the contents of your heart, you were judged and seen only through the lens of a diagnosis. You are a necessary and valuable member of the body, and the church *needs* you.

The tragic reality is that much of the church desperately needs to reframe its beliefs and preconceived notions about mental health. Not only do they need to be clothed in compassion, but they also need to be educated about all the various mental health challenges that affect one in

four individuals, whether or not they're believers.[2] Until
the church's misconceptions around mental health have
a serious come-to-Jesus moment, though, you may not
find the truth and compassion you're looking for within
certain Christian circles. However, no matter where you
find yourself, you *can* focus on the truth of God's character
as displayed repeatedly in the Bible. You *can* rest in how
God views and defines you, rather than letting your worth
come from the flawed beliefs of others.

Jesus and Therapy

Jesus

Ask God to show you where you've allowed others to assign your value or lack thereof. Pray for Him to begin a deep work of restoration in your heart as He reveals your true worth. Begin to separate the "Christ-like" people in your life whose words or actions don't reflect the actual character of Jesus Himself. The less the line between Christianity and Christ is blurred in your mind, the faster you'll see that Jesus doesn't want to hurt you, and that His arms are the safest place for you to be.

Therapy

If you have encountered people in your life who made you feel inferior, pinpoint those individuals and those instances with your therapist and look for ways you might have allowed their wounding messages to become part of your identity. Where have you internalized any blame or condemnation you've received? Have you taken ownership and carried the weight of a diagnosis that is out of your control?

Four

An Early Grave

Understanding and Responding to Suicidality

> He who has felt his own ruin will not imagine any to
> be hopeless; nor will he think them too fallen to be
> worthy of his regard.
>
> —CHARLES H. SPURGEON, "THE DESPISED FRIEND"

Trigger Warning: This chapter discusses the author's suicide attempt and suicidal ideation in detail. Some readers may find this upsetting. If you are struggling with these feelings, please let someone know and dial 988 for 24/7 confidential help from the 988 Suicide and Crisis Lifeline.

"I don't think I can do this anymore."

There, I'd said it. The truth was out there, again. At the height of my hopelessness, I battled constant thoughts about ending my life. My parents knew. My church leadership knew. Maybe this time, someone—anyone—would take my confession to heart, because I'd meant every word.

Looking up from my hands that were clenched in my lap, I prayed that this time would be different, that perhaps a buoy would be thrown to save me from the circumstances I was drowning in.

Say something! I screamed silently. *Help me!* But once again, the weight and management of my depression sat squarely on my own shoulders. No one made an appointment for me to see a doctor. No one suggested therapy as an option. No one saved me.

Instead of approaching me with pragmatic advice or tips for coping with my decline in mental health, people repeatedly told me to read my Bible more, to pray harder, and to meditate day and night on what is good. The message was clear: my depression and anxiety *weren't of God.* This further enforced the suggestion that the state of my mental health was a result of something I was doing wrong and that if I wanted to feel better, I could simply choose to heal.

Philippians 4:8 was drilled into me during that season. According to my mentors, it was the standard to measure every racing, chaotic, depressive thought against: "Finally, brothers and sisters, whatever is true, whatever is noble, whatever is right, whatever is pure, whatever is lovely, whatever is admirable—if anything is excellent or praiseworthy—think about such things" (NIV).

"Oh Tabitha, your thoughts about yourself aren't true."

Sure, despite the fact that my negative self-worth has been reinforced since infancy.

"Does what you think about Jesus sound right?!"

No . . . no, it does not. Finally, we agree on something.

"Is thinking about killing yourself admirable or praiseworthy?"

Of course not.

"Then snap out of it and stop thinking that way!"

Without the tools, emotional maturity, or psychiatric help I needed to navigate my circumstances, what was left of my fight dissipated. Ultimately, the abuse I'd experienced since birth, compounded by my parents' divorce, had led me to a new low in my depression with every passing year of my adolescence. At that point, I'd spent nearly half of my life grappling with the darkness, and I'd *never* won. I was tired and aged beyond my years and more than ready to leave the world behind.

(Note: I fully believe we're called to measure our thoughts against the Word of God, and you'll see that reflected throughout this book. God's Word is powerful, but it's not meant to be wielded as a tool to shame someone— someone a mental illness who needs treatment—into feeling guilty for symptoms of their diagnosis.)

Breaking Point

If I close my eyes, I can see the entire day of my suicide attempt play out like it was yesterday. I was almost sixteen years old. It was a beautiful Sunday morning as always. After all, in Hawaii I lived in "paradise." I'd walked into my church's sanctuary and found a spot in the middle of a back row. As one of my favorite worship leaders sang, tears streamed down my face. For once, I didn't try to stop them. I'd already been labeled as an unacceptable Christian, so why bother putting on a happy face? It didn't matter what I did or what I said, I'd be judged. It didn't matter how much pain I was in, no one was coming to save me.

I cried through the entire service and not a soul approached me. To this day, I wonder if things might have gone differently if someone had stopped—stopped faking it, stopped brushing past people's very real pain and grief, stopped pretending that God expected us to always be fine. I'll never know. As I walked out of that service, it was as if someone had sapped the oxygen from the room. Gulping for air, I pushed past the familiar faces milling around the pews. If I had anything to say about it, I'd never see any of them again, and as far as I knew, not one of them would care.

I walked home and went into my room. Shaking from fear at what I was about to do, I wept as I paced my bedroom's worn carpet. It wasn't until I felt only a gaping emptiness inside that the tears finally stopped. Picking up the bottle of pills, I wondered if my chosen method of taking my life would hurt. Would I experience further trauma and wake up in a hospital bed? Or would I just drift off peacefully to wherever I was headed? Quite frankly, at the moment, my destination felt like a toss-up between Heaven and Hell.

I poured a handful of medication into my left hand and downed the tiny pills with a glass of water. I don't remember how quickly I passed out, but somehow, I managed to climb into my bed before the blackness took over. Since I'd heavily relied on sleep as an escape from my dark thoughts throughout the severe depressive episodes of the past year, I was counting on the fact that no one would find it unusual that I was "asleep" in the late afternoon. By the time someone realized what I'd done, I needed it to be too late to intervene.

Signs of Suicidality

Josie Rosenberg, a behavioral health counselor, said, "It's hopelessness—that's the main link with suicide. When someone considers suicide, they have no cognitive flexibility. They are unable to see other options or possibilities. They are stuck and believe this is the *only* solution for problems, problems that could very likely be solved if they get help."[3]

Unfortunately, far too many things can lead to suicidal ideation, including:

- Mental health conditions, including anxiety, depression, PTSD, and bipolar disorder
- Ongoing pain
- Heavy stress
- Family history of suicide
- Illegal drug use
- Past trauma or abuse
- A recent tragedy or death[4]

According to one survey, 12.2 percent of 18- to 25-year-olds responded affirmatively to the question, "At any time in the past twelve months, did you seriously think about trying to kill yourself?"[5]

For people with mental health disorders, the rate is *significantly higher.* The exact numbers are unclear, but since suicidal ideation is a symptom of mental health disorders like major depression and bipolar disorder, the problem exists at a far greater percentage in these populations.[6]

If you've walked a journey similar to mine, you're likely already familiar with the signs listed below, but in case you're concerned about a loved one and/or are unfamiliar with what losing hope can feel like, here are some warning signs that someone may be contemplating suicide:

- Isolating from loved ones
- Feeling hopeless or trapped
- Talking about death or suicide
- Giving away possessions
- An increase in substance use or misuse
- Increased mood swings, anger, rage, and/or irritability
- Engaging in risk-taking behavior
- Accessing the means to kill oneself, such as medication, drugs, or a firearm
- Acting as if they're saying goodbye to people
- Feeling extremely anxious

If you suspect that a loved one is thinking about or planning suicide, ask them about it directly. I think few people in my life truly thought I would follow through with my constant ideations. Maybe by that point, my depression was "the norm" and had been accepted as a part of who I was. I cannot recall a single occurrence of a lay person or anyone in leadership in my church bringing up mental health in a discussion, sermon, or Bible study, and maybe my family thought that to discuss my persistent suicidal thoughts would be to encourage them. But it's a myth that your concern will give another person the idea to kill themselves. On the contrary, asking shows that you're concerned and that you care.

Be aware that passive suicidal ideation, such as wishing you could die in your sleep or in an accident rather than by your own hand, is not necessarily any less serious than active suicidal ideation. It can quickly turn active, and it most certainly has a blend of active and passive components. Take anyone's thoughts about suicide seriously. And seek help if *you* are having them.[7]

Still Here

I woke up on my own the morning after my suicide attempt. I can only interpret that by saying that God must have decided it wasn't my time yet. Graced with the mother of all headaches, it took me a while to come to and realize I'd survived. As reality sunk in, a feeling of explosive rage flooded through me. I had tried and failed to escape the hell on earth I was living in. After stewing for a while, I finally conceded that since I was still in the land of the living, I might as well get up and go to my job at the church-run school where I worked. Ditching my shift would only create more problems I didn't have the strength to face.

I had no mental framework for how to act normally that day. It was just a Monday for all my other coworkers, and there I was, still feeling hungover from my overdose. Though I wanted to die more than I wanted to live, some survival instinct nudged me to confide in a coworker about what I'd done. Very few people were on shift that afternoon, and there was no rhyme or reason to my decision to confess my attempted suicide to my energetic Australian workmate. And when my coworker relayed my confession to my mom, it went about as well as you can imagine. She panicked. Any semblance of independence I'd been granted was gone. I was no longer trusted to be alone or even to lock my door. All the pain meds in the apartment were hidden. Everything shifted toward my immediate safety. Still, no changes were made that would support my overall well-being in the long term. The root causes of my pain weren't addressed, and the very abusive behavior and people who had driven me to take my life were still alive and well.

Now that I am a parent, it's not hard to envision how I'd react if my child attempted suicide. If you asked my fourteen-year-old daughter how I would respond if I felt she were in danger, she'd likely tell you that I'd handcuff us together—and that wouldn't be too far from the truth! I would move heaven and earth to protect my children. But as a teenager drowning in depression, all I wanted was someone to calm the storms around me, rather than (justifiably) panic and take away what very little control I already had over my privacy and autonomy.

Responding to Someone Who Is Suicidal

Sadly, suicide is the third leading cause of death for people ages 15-25, and roughly five hundred thousand people commit suicide each year.[8] The tragic suicide of a young pastor, whom we will talk about more, is what spurred me to write this book to begin with. After countless conversations, I've realized how ill-equipped many Christians feel when it comes to suicide and suicidal ideation. Understandably, it is uncomfortable for some. There is also a fear associated with the potential repercussions of not saying or doing the "right" thing. So how should we respond as Christians to someone who is suicidal? No two situations are the same, but I believe we should always . . .

- Take peoples' threats seriously. Accompany them to get help if necessary.

- Access their home life and situation. Is there immediate danger or unsafe circumstances (such as abuse occurring within the home) that need to be reported?
- Offer a listening ear and listen with the intent to understand what led to this point of desperation.
- Connect them with mental health resources if they are not already receiving care.
- Show that they are valuable to you and plead with them to stay.
- Remind them of the love God has for them but refrain from preaching at them.

Suicide: No One Is Immune

A husband and father of two young boys, Jarrid Wilson was a beloved pastor at Harvest Christian Fellowship in Riverside, California. He was also a passionate mental health advocate who founded Anthem of Hope to help others like himself who struggled with depression. He continually brought the plight of his and others' mental health struggles to light. Shortly after officiating the service of a young woman who had killed herself, he shook his family and friends by committing suicide. His last post read, "Loving Jesus doesn't always cure suicidal thoughts."[9]

Andrew Stoecklein was the lead pastor of Inland Hills Church in California when he, at just thirty years old, took his life. His wife, Kayla, was left with the task of informing their three sons, their friends, their congregation, and the world of his passing. She wrote, "Last night, the love of my life, the father of my children and the pastor of our incredible church took his last breath and went to be with Jesus. It wasn't the miracle I was hoping for but he is now in heaven with his dad, free of pain, free of depression and anxiety."[10]

Both Jarrid's and Andrew's widows have become avid mental health advocates and continue to carry on their husbands' legacies, proof that beautiful things can come from brokenness. Jarrid's and Andrew's untimely deaths impacted me greatly. Many close friends of mine are in ministry, and I often have a front-row seat to their struggles. They carry a weight few of us can imagine, yet who can they lean on? Who can they confide in? While you'll hear me call on the church to advocate for mental health, it's not only those in the pews who need help. It's those behind the pulpit as well.

Only Human

The body of Christ has lost too many like Jarrid and Andrew to suicide, while many other church leaders have suffered both public and private mental health crises. And though these tragedies always seem to stir an initial conversation, they are too quickly forgotten. We can lose sight of the fact that people in our congregation and sphere of influence are still struggling with their mental health every day *and* that pastors are people as well, susceptible to the same ailments as the rest of humanity. *All* these individuals need the church to be a safe place where they can be open about their struggles and not be ostracized, shamed, or judged.

If you are an individual in church leadership who is battling depression, anxiety, or some other form of mental health struggle, you face challenges and pressure that are unique to ministry. As such, you must safeguard your mental health in different ways. Here are five beneficial repetitive things you can do to avoid burnout:

1. **Find a counselor and make friendships outside of your church.** This creates a safe space for you to feel that you can be authentic without jeopardizing your position or having fear of judgment or gossip.

2. **Consider being honest with your congregation.** Though some individuals may make thoughtless or inappropriate comments, your transparency can be part of changing the narrative behind mental health. In the end, you may be surprised to discover who supports you and how many lives you change by opening up the conversation and normalizing this struggle.

3. **Carve out time to care for your mental health.** It is not realistic for you to be available 24/7 to your congregation. There will always be people in need of ministry, but Jesus modeled stepping away from the crowd to spend time with His Father, and what better example to follow? Schedule time to unplug on a regular basis—and make sure you do it.

4. **Take a Sabbath.** Just as we offer our 10 percent tithe and trust God to make the other 90 percent enough, give God that one day to refresh your soul and trust that He will make the other six days of the week enough to complete the things you need to do.

5. **Maintain your walk with Christ.** Before you're a pastor, you are a child of God. Maintaining a vibrant walk with Christ through spiritual disciplines is a key component of sustaining your mental health.[11]

Author and pastor Michael Cooper explained the benefits of church leaders talking about the struggles they are facing:

> As pastors, we maintain a level of confidentiality with those we serve. We vow not to discuss their problems with others while praying for them in private. Sometimes, however, we take this to the extreme and fail to discuss our own problems. We must be willing to open up and talk to people about our struggles. By doing so, we verbalize our pain and speak what we feel. Personally, this is one of the most helpful ways I've found to manage mental health. I tend to suppress how I feel until I explode. This is why I confide in my pastor and seek his wisdom. Some may also seek professional counseling. *There's no shame in this at all.* We all need help and—praise the Lord—there are people who desire to help.[12] (Emphasis Added)

Let It Begin with Me

Regretfully, I have yet to speak with a person who felt their church was adequately addressing the mental health conversation. If you're a pastor—or if you're in church leadership—*you* can be part of the change that needs to happen. According to a recent poll, 49 percent of pastors rarely or never address mental health from the pulpit. By contrast, a whopping 76 percent of churchgoers say suicide is a problem in their community that needs to be addressed.[13]

If you are a pastor who's realizing that you've mishandled one or more of your members' mental health struggles, or perhaps failed to address this problem area at all, let's talk about four ways you can move forward to be a part of the solution in your own church:

1. **Take ownership.** If you have mishandled the topic of mental health, one of the most freeing and important things you can do is apologize to the people you might have wounded. Owning how you got it wrong, whether it was your intention or not, is always the right thing to do. How the recipient responds to your apology is up to them, but in the eyes of God, you will have done what you can, as far as it depends on you.

2. **Get educated.** The very next thing I hope you will do is educate yourself on mental health. We will be walking through the specifics of various diagnoses throughout this book. I hope you'll pay close attention with the intent to gain a deeper understanding of how these challenges can impact someone's daily life and how to best support those living with a mental health diagnosis.

3. **Offer outside resources.** Aside from simply getting educated yourself, another helpful thing any pastor can do is refer out for counseling. It takes humility to recognize when someone you are speaking with needs a deeper level of care than you have the expertise to offer. The kindest thing you can do for them—and the best way you can serve them—is to refer them to someone who *is* qualified to help them walk through the issues they are facing. This might quite literally mean the difference between life and death.

4. **Attend trainings.** Lastly, one of my primary recommendations is for your entire staff to attend workshops that will raise awareness and participate in sensitivity training for how to appropriately interact with individuals struggling with mental health challenges. The ones I recommend have been carefully curated by my friends at Speak Out PDX. They host workshops

that involve a team of psychologists, therapists, pastors, and their nonprofit's director, which are intended to give you the best well-rounded overview of psychoeducation and biblical principles.

As my story and the stories of so many others illustrate, we, as the body of Christ, are missing the mark when it comes to mental health. It is time for the church to change course. It is time to address the growing crisis in our midst. It is time to educate ourselves on how to respond lovingly to our neighbors with mental health disorders. It is time to create resource packets to be handed out as freely as we give away Bibles. It is time to accept our limitations and develop a network of trusted counselors for referral. It is time for us to ditch the hushed tones and speak openly and honestly about depression, anxiety, and suicide from the pulpit.

The mental health crisis is escalating, and it is here—in our youth ministry, in the smiling faces that grace our sanctuaries, in the people behind the pulpit, and in the broken spirits of those who have denounced their faith. As believers, we should be first on the front lines—a loving, comforting community that embraces individuals in their deepest hour of need and shows them Jesus. All of us have the responsibility to help stop the spread of false narratives that harm an already vulnerable people group and start spreading more of the love and hope of Jesus.

Jesus and Therapy

Jesus

Have you taken part in wounding someone with your words or perhaps spoken something over someone in God's name that wasn't reflective of His heart and truth? Ask Jesus to illuminate any area where you need to change your perspective on those who suffer from suicidal thoughts and any area where He is calling you to go in and *be* the change in the body of Christ.

Therapy

Whether you're the individual who is suicidal or you're trying to help someone who is, it's a heavy load to bear. You shouldn't go through this hardship alone. I encourage you to have a counselor who can carry the weight with you and support you. If you find yourself in a mental health crisis, please reach out to one of the phone numbers or websites listed in the back of this book.

Five

Jesus and Therapy

Dismantling False Beliefs About Christians and Mental Health

> "'Faith without works is dead.' Likewise, taking
> care of our mental health means being prayerful
> and being practical."
>
> —BRITTNEY MOSES, *SPEAKING OUR MINDS* PODCAST

If there was a silver lining to my suicide attempt, it was that my parents finally recognized that I needed to go to therapy. I should have been in counseling for nearly a decade, but better late than never, right? A big deal was made out of specifically finding a Christian therapist, so of course the man I began seeing was a Christian counselor. Dr. G had earned his doctorate in psychology the year I was born, so I figured he had vast experience under his belt and knew what he was doing.

I wasn't sure what to expect at counseling, but I still remember sitting in the psychologist's office responding to pages and pages of questions. The more questions I answered, the more I realized the depth of my emotional and mental health issues. *I mean . . . is anyone really surprised by this point?* Although it typically takes a few sessions when beginning counseling to cover a patient's history, I feel like it took at least two months of sessions to even begin to explain my life from birth to age sixteen. It was such a relief to finally be talking to an adult who validated my experiences, without dismissing or denying what I'd lived through.

Up to this point, I'd carried the weight of my painful circumstances alone, despite not being the one who had made a single decision that caused them. But every Friday afternoon, I could curl up in the recliner facing Dr. G, in whatever colorful Hawaiian shirt he was wearing for Aloha Friday (it's a thing in the islands—don't ask me to explain it!), and for the first time my pain was validated by someone who didn't respond in anger or make me feel guilty. That office was the only place I didn't have to communicate my pain perfectly, hide my anger, or tie a pretty bow on the ugly truth, because it was too messy.

I recall after telling Dr. G that I no longer wanted to be a Christian, he told me he would work with me on processing my trauma experienced in church and help me deal with the fallout. I told him more about my pain and what I thought I wanted, and he helped me make a road map to guide myself out of the mess I was in. Finally, a grown-up who understood that I was not the problem child I'd been made out to be. I was just a kid—a broken, hurting, mistreated, and abused kid who'd finally found the help she needed.

I would be remiss to not mention that while many believers have a requirement that their counselors be Christian, some of my most effective therapists were not, by definition, "Christian counselors," even if they themselves *were* people of faith.

While I certainly understand an individual's desire to see a therapist who shares their belief system, psychiatric help is psychiatric help, and if you or a loved one is in a situation where you need immediate mental health care, it would be better to at least get in the door with someone and start to work on some basic coping and stress management skills, or get on some medication if necessary, while still keeping the door open for finding a good Christian counselor down the road, if that is your desire. I have talked to many people who feel like it must be a Christian therapist, or they won't see anyone. While I cannot tell you how to feel, if someone you love is talking about suicide, please get *whatever help* is available to them, because their life hangs in the balance.

The Benefits of Jesus and Therapy

My experience with Dr. G was the start of a lifelong appreciation of the benefits of therapy. According to one study, therapy is helpful for about 75 percent of people who try it.[14] That's a pretty decent success rate, don't you think? Thankfully, in my case, I fell within that percentage of people who benefit from talking to a trusted professional. To say therapy was life-changing for me is no exaggeration. For what seemed like the first time in my life, I had compassionate acknowledgment of my pain, clear and unbiased guidance and support, and an adult in my corner who didn't require me to always be the bigger person—to stifle my needs and feelings to allow them to feel OK about their actions that had caused my pain.

Whether you're battling a mental health condition or simply need someone to talk to in a difficult season, regular therapy comes with many benefits, such as improvements in symptoms and quality of life. Anyone needing guidance or a listening ear during a stressful life event can profit from attending counseling sessions. If you have questions about how to find a therapist, please refer to the resources section at the back of this book.

Potential benefits of therapy include:

- Strengthened communication skills
- Better sleep
- Increased happiness and life satisfaction
- Greater feelings of empowerment; improved mental function and productivity; fewer missed days from school or work
- Improved relationships and interactions with other people
- Enhanced physical well-being, such as lower blood pressure or reduction in chronic pain
- Expanded development of skills for coping with daily life challenges and stress
- Improved management of behavioral health challenges, such as reducing or quitting smoking or drinking alcohol[15]

During my time in therapy with Dr. G, one of the most powerful things for me was having my clinical depression and anxiety validated as a legitimate medical issue, rather than tying it to my faith or lack thereof. In many Christian circles, there is a preconceived notion that having a troubled mind following trauma, grief, and other abuse is purely a spiritual matter. This over-spiritualization of mental illness and failure to recognize the very real psychosomatic issues at play perpetuates a false narrative. Experiencing inherent brokenness, whether physical or mental, is not an indicator of our belief in Jesus. The idea that we should be ashamed of our struggles or that we are somehow to blame for them is a lie perpetuated by those who do not understand that we live in a fallen world.

One of the gravest mistakes many Christians have made is to create a partition between how we follow Jesus and our steps to receive treatment for mental health struggles, as if the two cannot go hand in hand. The subsequent shame historically associated with these struggles has resulted in us losing far too many to the darkness because we failed to create a safe space for them to bring their hardships into the light. In my case, and based on my many conversations with others, these false beliefs are what push a majority of hurting people away from actively attending church or having a relationship with God at all.

We need to accept the fact that the brain is part of the body and, as such, is susceptible to sickness, pain, and trauma in this fallen world. The wise Charles Spurgeon wrote in his commentary on Psalm 88, "The mind can descend far lower than the body, for in it there are bottomless pits. The flesh can bear only a certain number of wounds, and no more, but the soul can bleed in ten thousand ways, and die over and over again each hour."

Because the brain is an organ, it can malfunction and cause us pain and trouble just as much as any other internal organ that fails to function properly.

As members of the faith community, if we take no issue with treating the body for sickness and injury, shouldn't we apply that same mentality to those suffering emotionally? Instead of holding on to preconceptions that alienate and damage those struggling with mental health, shouldn't we continue to normalize discussions about our mental health and well-being and combat the double standards some Christians hold related to this topic?

Misconceptions About Mental Health

The problem with being indoctrinated with a flawed perspective, especially at an early age, is that falsehoods become your core beliefs. After hearing them stated as truth for so long and replaying the words repeatedly in your mind, the lies eventually become the predominant voice in your head. It can be so difficult to go back and uproot those deep-seated beliefs about yourself, but it *can* be done.

In this chapter and the next, I'm going to walk you through some of the most common misconceptions about mental health within the church, along with suggested examples of how to respond if you find yourself on the receiving end of any of these fallacies. These potential responses will give you something to fall back on if you find yourself in a situation where you freeze up, unable to believe someone just said something so misguided or untrue about you and your mental health.

While I try not to be too snarky when responding to outdated and flawed misperceptions related to mental health and Christianity, I am sure to be firm, educational, and biblical. What the recipient does with that information is neither my nor your responsibility. If you've corrected the misinformation, drawn your line in the sand, and clearly defined what you are or are not OK with discussing, they are less likely to press the issue. Once you state your case, be proud of yourself and then move on!

False Belief #1: Your Faith Is Weak if You Have a Mental Health Diagnosis

Oh, my friends, absolutely nothing could be further from the truth. You have endured so much struggle, wrestled with so many doubts, but you're still here believing that despite everything you see around you, God is with you and you are worthy of His love. You might be barely holding on to the remnants of your faith, but the fact that you've endured all the hurtful things done to you in God's name and you're still searching for the Jesus you hope is out there—that's strength. That is a faith many of the Pharisees who have mistreated you may never understand.

You can believe in Jesus with your whole heart but still wrestle with suicidal thoughts. Even if you faithfully follow the Lord, you may still have daily panic attacks. Your faith being the foundation of your life doesn't erase your diagnosis. Please hear me: *your mental health struggle is in no way, shape, or form an indication of a shallow faith in God.* In fact, I genuinely believe you have some of the deepest and strongest faith of all because trusting and holding on to Jesus in the dark places that mental health diagnoses can take you to is not for the weak of heart.

A Moment for Mending

Take some time to forgive yourself for all the instances where you have been unkind to yourself for not being stronger or for not believing in God without wrestling with doubt. God sees your heart and your faith. There is nothing left to prove. Declare this verse aloud or memorize it for those moments when you're feeling like your faith or standing with God is being challenged: "We are made right with God by placing our faith in Jesus Christ. And this is true for everyone who believes, no matter who we are" (Romans 3:22 NLT).

Potential Responses to Your Faith Being Challenged:

Response #1: In 1 Kings 18, Elijah prayed *fire* down from Heaven and then, one chapter later, asked God to take his life because he was so disappointed and distraught at his circumstances. If a prophet whom God used to perform *sixteen* miracles and speak to kings can experience depression, I'm quite sure that my mental health struggles don't tarnish my faith in the eyes of God.

Response #2: The Bible tells us that giants in the faith, such as David, Moses, Naomi, Job, Jonah, Jeremiah, and Elijah, wrestled with deep despair, loneliness, and sadness. Nowhere does scripture denounce them for having weak faith. In fact, they were used mightily by God, so I'm OK being in their company.

False Belief #2: If You Seek Professional Help, You're Not Trusting God

Is God all-powerful and mighty to save? Absolutely. He can do anything, but He often chooses to work through flesh and blood to carry out His divine purposes on earth.

If you were having a heart attack, wouldn't you want to see a cardiologist, an expert in the field, to understand what was going on with your heart? And if you broke your leg, wouldn't you head straight to an orthopedist who had the knowledge and tools to help you heal with the best possible outcome? When we deal with physical injuries, we know where to go—to the experienced medical professionals trained to address our ailment. When it comes to mental health, our approach should be the same. For the best possible outcome, we need the appropriate mental health specialist with the knowledge, skill, and training to help us with our specific condition.

While there are wonderful pastors who do helpful and effective counseling, those of us who wrestle with our mental health often need more specialized attention. I'm not saying that church leadership is always unequipped to handle some of your counseling and be a part of your support system. However, sometimes you simply need an expert in your corner. Thankfully, our medical system is full of them.

There's a story about a man who was waiting on his roof as the floodwaters rose. He was praying to God for help when a man in a rowboat came by and said, "Jump in, I can save you." The stranded gentleman declined and said, "It's OK. I am praying to God, and He's going to save me." Next, a motorboat came by and made the same offer to save the man from drowning, but the response was the same: "No, thanks. I am praying to God. I have faith that He'll save me." Finally, a helicopter hovered over him and threw down a rope to lift the stranded man to safety, but he refused to grab on, convinced that God was going to answer his prayers and save him. The man drowned and, when he arrived in Heaven, he told God, "I had faith in You, but You did not save me. I do not understand why." God replied, "I sent you a rowboat, a motorboat, and a helicopter. What else did you expect?"

This story so perfectly illustrates the lack of wisdom in choosing to suffer as we wait for a supernatural solution. Yet why would we stay trapped in the rising floodwaters when God has called and equipped amazing counselors, psychiatrists, psychologists, and clinical social workers to help draw us out? Some of the most genuine and compassionate people I know are in these professions, and God has used them as a lifeline to keep me from drowning more times than I can count. I trust God deeply, but when it comes to the hard work of healing, He often calls me to move my feet. There are specific events I need to heal from, forgiveness I need to work on, coping mechanisms I need to develop, and steps I need to take to be as healthy and whole as possible. None of that inner work diminishes my trust in the Lord.

A Moment for Mending

Who has God sent to draw you out of the floodwaters? Is there a step you need to take to receive help? Has shame, fear, or embarrassment kept you from reaching out to a counselor or psychiatrist? You don't have to silently struggle any longer. Help is waiting, and in the back of this book, you will find a list of mental health resources, along with suggested ministries, podcasts, and phone numbers for you to easily access when you need them.

Potential Responses to Combating Arguments Against Seeking Professional Help:

Response #1: Throughout my life, I have met some of the most amazing believers who just happened to be in the helping professions, whether doctors, police officers, teachers, counselors, pastors, nurses, or social workers. Why would God equip them with a special skill set and allow them to operate in their calling and purpose, but condemn me for utilizing their God-given gift?

Response #2: I trust God with my whole heart, but if I'm having a heart attack, I'm heading to the hospital. If someone breaks into my house, I'm calling 911. In the same way, if my mind is troubled to the point that I can no longer cope, I'm calling a therapist. God is clear in Scripture that He made us for community, fellowship, and for one another. Just as each part of our physical body plays a role in our overall health, each of us has a function within the body of Christ that we are meant to fulfill to contribute to the well-being of the church as a whole. So, why would seeking help be looked down upon by God if He specifically gifted people in the field of psychology? If God gifted these professionals to help me understand what is going on in my mind and emotions, you better believe I'm utilizing their gifts! Just as no one would think twice about going to a trusted friend for advice, a professional counselor or therapist typically offers the same benefit but with the added bonus of confidentiality, education, and, hopefully, a tremendous amount of relevant experience.

False Belief #3: If You Prayed More, You Wouldn't Need Medication

I've been told more than a few times over the decades that if I just prayed a little harder, I wouldn't need to take medication for my anxiety or depression. I'll be honest—I don't love taking medication for anything. If there is a trick, tip, vitamin, or exercise I can do instead of popping a pill, count me in! If prayer were going to offset my need for medication in some seasons of life, I think it would have worked already because I already *do* pray without ceasing—okay, very little ceasing. My prayers may not be elaborate or impressive, but I've made it a habit through my entire walk with the Lord to talk to Him consistently. He is my counselor, my Father, my defender, my best friend.

Despite my constant conversations with Jesus, I was told I wouldn't have anxiety if I surrendered my worries to Him and trusted Him.

Have you ever had a debilitating panic attack that stifled your ability to watch your kids while they're at sports practice, stay on the road while driving to work, or even take in enough oxygen to keep yourself from passing out? It starts with a racing heart. You're fairly sure you're having a heart attack. Then you can't catch your breath. No matter how hard you try, it feels like there is a hole somewhere that's letting all your air out. Then come the tremors that eventually become such violent shakes, onlookers might think you're having a seizure. While everyone's panic attacks may not look the same, there are certainly similar elements to many of them. More than a few times, I have been found balled up on the floor, sobbing and shaking uncontrollably. Unresolved trauma has a funny way of sneaking up on you and, as author Bessel van der Kolk states, "The body keeps the score."[16]

Thanks to years of walking with Jesus and receiving therapy, I know all the self-soothing exercises to implement in a pending crisis. Not a day goes by that I don't bring my anxiety before the Lord. I trust Jesus, but when I reach a point where I'm incapacitated and unable to care for my children, prayer is not the only weapon I'm turning to. I'm going to take hold of the lifeboat at hand—a prescribed and carefully monitored medication to calm my nervous system down.

Can you imagine taking an oxygen mask off someone who's on life support and demanding that they breathe on their own? Similarly, if someone is facing a mental health crisis, is their medicine a "crutch" if it's necessary to their functionality or could even save their life?

A Moment for Mending

Work toward coming to peace with your body and its needs. Just as a diabetic may always require insulin, there might be a medication that you need to keep taking if it aids you in functioning normally. You are not failing God because your nervous system doesn't cope as "well" as your neighbor's. You are not doing anything wrong by filling a prescription and taking that medication. You are acting responsibly to care for your body in the best way that you—and the professionals who are helping you—know how.

Potential Responses to Arguments Against Taking Medication:

Response #1: You know how you take Tylenol when you have a headache or Benadryl when you are having an allergic reaction? Do you feel that taking those medications diminishes your faith and trust in God? I don't either! If God has given people the wisdom to create medicine that will help our bodies function as they were designed to in this broken world, I'm grateful. That is precisely how I see mental health medications: they help my mind and body operate as God intended them to.

Response #2: If a medication helped someone keep their heartbeat stable or their blood sugar regular, would you suggest they stop taking it? Your statement implies that my condition isn't as biological as those very real physical conditions. If you'd like, I'd be happy to sit down with you and help you understand how things like chemical imbalances, trauma, or even environmental factors can cause legitimate physical damage to our brains.

Response #3: Whether I'm on medication or not is between my doctor and myself. As I'm sure you can understand, it's not something I'm willing to discuss.

It Can Get Better

If you found yourself nodding along and resonating with some of these unhealthy viewpoints and wondering if you can ever heal from the damage they caused in your life, I'm living proof you can. There is *so* much hope and healing in counseling, prayer, medication, emotional support, and addressing past trauma. If you find yourself overwhelmed about your future and how your diagnosis might impact it, I cannot tell you that it won't have some bearing on it. But I can tell you that you *can* get to a better place and that many treatment options are available as you walk toward healing.

As you navigate this journey, I pray you will rest in the assurance that you are so much more than your diagnosis (or diagnoses). If you need to reach out for help, please do! There is absolutely nothing to be ashamed of in asking for assistance. Jesus is not at war with mental health professionals. You can walk hand in hand with both Jesus and a therapist. In fact, you are doing the bravest thing of all by allowing someone in who can walk you through the hard things. We were never meant to go on this journey alone.

Jesus and Therapy

Jesus

Thank the Lord for giving you the wisdom and courage to seek out help and good advice when you need it and for gifting so many people with the understanding and desire—and professional training—to help walk people through mental health issues.

Therapy

If you've been criticized for attending therapy, utilizing medication, or even for simply having a diagnosis, ask your therapist to help you process those false beliefs so you can release any hold they still have over you. Know that you are being brave and doing the hard work of healing, and that deserves to be celebrated, not shamed!

Six

The Fall from Grace

Separating Christ from Christianity

> God cannot give us happiness and peace apart
> from Himself, because it is not there. There is no
> such thing.
>
> —C. S. LEWIS, *MERE CHRISTIANITY*

*Trigger Warning: This chapter discusses self-harm and spiritual
abuse.*

As I neared my sixteenth birthday, there was only one
thing I thought I knew, and it was that Christianity and I
were not compatible. I could not find a way to fit in with
Christians, to accept their smiling, "everything is fine"
fronts. I did not belong to their club, and I was too weary
to jump through the rings of fire they kept holding before
me to prove I was a worthy Christ follower. I'd been torn
down one too many times by them, and I wasn't about to
subject myself to that again. I was done.

"Mom, would you rather have me be happy or be a
Christian?" I asked her one evening as we sat in the quiet
of our living room. "Because I can't be both."

I vividly recall her telling me that happiness was only temporary. "Of course, I would *like* for you to be happy, but I would *rather* you have eternal life," she said.

I stared at the corner of the room, seeing absolutely nothing as I processed that there was no way I was coming out of this *not* being a failure in everyone's mind, including my mom's. As I'd confessed to her, having a relationship with Jesus no longer felt like a viable option for me. I couldn't untangle myself from all the trauma I'd experienced in the church, and I had no emotional energy left to sort out what was and wasn't of God. If I walked away from my faith, literally all the people I knew would be disappointed in me. But if I stayed it would be the death of me.

My belief in God's goodness was gone, and my belief in His existence was waning. Even as I was recovering from my first suicide attempt, I was planning my next one. I was numb, and any natural instinct to protect myself or preserve my life was gone. Thanks to my dwindling mental state, I was headed down a slippery slope. Determined to numb the pain that consumed every waking moment, I began overdosing on whatever over-the-counter pain medications I could get my hands on and cutting my wrists.

I was still forced to attend my childhood church, and it was making me sick—physically, emotionally, and spiritually. I hated being there, surrounded by people who'd already made it clear how worthless I was to them. My self-harm always followed a church service, which probably tells you everything you need to know.

During one evening service, Abe, the pastor, demanded to prophesy over me again. Once again, I was directed to sit in the chair of doom in the middle of the room. I felt powerless to stop him. I didn't want *anyone* to speak over me ever again. I didn't want *anyone* to lay hands on me ever again. I didn't want to be surrounded by hypocrites with arms outstretched, using their "words from the Lord" to proclaim curses over my life.

I'm already cursed—you won, I thought bitterly.

Feeling powerless to fight back, I lowered myself to the chair like the obedient church girl I'd been trained to be, even as my insides churned. Despite my fight-or-flight instinct being on fire, I dutifully sat stone-faced, tears silently rolling down my cheeks. Perhaps Abe thought God was using him to minister to me, but in reality, I was dying inside, my skin crawling in revulsion at his touch and his words.

Everything inside of me screamed to get out of there, so as soon as Abe was done speaking, I got up and started speed walking toward the exit, choking back sobs. I ran crying down the dead-end road lined with warehouses where the church was located. Finally stopping at the sight of the broken beer bottles that littered the ground, I picked up a dirty, jagged shard of glass and started cutting. Perhaps I thought I could bleed out some of the pain that was always trapped in my body and mind. I was in absolute anguish, but I couldn't go home. Pulling my sleeves down over my bloody wrists, I wiped my tears and stifled all my emotions like I always did. Then I walked back to the church and into the service because there was nowhere else for me to go. I didn't know a single other person on that island who was not also a church member, so there was no safe haven for me. That church was my whole world, whether I liked it or not.

After a while, I started to think that maybe the abuse I'd experienced was just isolated to my church and that if I could simply get away from it, things would get better. So,

I begged my mother for permission to leave my childhood church and find a new one. I knew there was no way I'd be allowed to leave church altogether, yet I was trying to find some compromise to get away from the environment that was turning me further away from Jesus. I think somewhere deep in my heart, I was searching for a way to not just throw in the towel on my faith but find somewhere I'd be accepted and feel safe. My request was denied, and I was told as long as I was under my mom's roof, I would have no choice but to attend the same church.

Despite all the obvious damage the church had done—from my shattered self-esteem and declining physical and mental health to my ever-growing PTSD—it was determined that I *could* and *would* forgive these men and stay in that particular church "family." Abe's solution to my dilemma was to insist that I meet with him, my mother, and other witnesses so I could forgive them.

My heart cried out, *God, I can't forgive them. I just can't. They are not even remotely sorry. They have no idea the magnitude of collateral damage they always leave behind. Please don't let them corner me again, confuse me again, blame me again. Please protect me—please.*

I was taught as a young girl that the Bible commands you to forgive as Christ has forgiven you, and now I was being told once again that it would be wrong for me to not at least sit and listen to my abusers and hear them out. Apparently, they weren't done gaslighting or emotionally manipulating the minor in their midst.

To this day, I can hear the weak explanations that came next and the futile attempts to excuse their abusive actions with their good intentions. I could feel my heart getting more jaded by the moment. The goal of the meeting had nothing to do with repentance and everything to do with sweeping their sins under the rug. They didn't want *me* to tarnish *their* image. Once again, they were driving me away from any desire to continue being a Christian.

Finally, the day came when I'd absolutely had it. I put my foot down and adamantly refused to ever set foot in that church again.

"That's it!" I told my mom. "I am not going to this church anymore—period. I'll still go to church, but the one of my choosing. And unless you are going to physically drag me there, last week was my *last* Sunday at your church!"

Oh, the irony that now I finally sounded like the rebellious teenager I'd been labeled as for years! But I was tired of constantly fighting to be heard, protected, and loved. If I was going to continue functioning on a daily basis, I couldn't keep suppressing the magnitude of emotions I was facing. I had to remove myself from that environment if I was ever going to be healthy as an individual. I had to stop being fed a steady diet of lies about the heart and the character of God long enough to discern His voice from all the others who supposedly were speaking on His behalf.

The Lies That Bind and the Truth That Sets Free

To help you make the same differentiation that I eventually made between Christ and Christians, we'll be breaking down three more detrimental false beliefs. The inaccurate representation of Jesus in my life led me to spend countless years on the outside looking in, wishing God's grace was for me.

As you read some of these lies, which you might have been told as well, my prayer is that the truth of how God really feels about you sinks into every fiber of your heart and mind. May His voice be louder than the world's deception as you allow His truth to penetrate the deeply wounded parts of your soul. May His love draw you closer toward the healing and wholeness He wants for you.

False Belief #4: Depression Is a Punishment from God

How the concept of depression as divine punishment came to be is anyone's guess, as there is no biblical ground for God afflicting someone with depression. In fact, the word *depression* is never actually used in the Bible at all, though you will find words such as *downcast*, *miserable*, *despairing*, or *mourning* in scripture.

God's Word informs us that He does not delight in punishing us. In fact, James 1:17 tells us that every good and perfect gift comes from our Heavenly Father. Lamentations 3:33 goes as far as to say that He does not willingly bring suffering or affliction on His children. In other words, God is not looking for ways to cause us pain. He is not observing our comings and goings in hopes of finding the one area we messed up in so He can swoop in and discipline us.

Does God use our grief, sadness, and brokenness for His good and somehow redeem our mistakes? Absolutely! Is He the *cause* of your mental anguish? I assure you—He is not. God sees all and knows all, so He knew that your story would include these hard parts. While He would never orchestrate a situation in which you would be hurt, abused, or abandoned, or experience whatever pain may have occurred in your life, He did already know about what would happen before time began. He has always had a plan to put your broken pieces back together to form a beautiful mosaic that would testify to His grace.

A Moment for Mending

This lie that depression is a divine punishment is not shaken off easily. It takes a lot of intentional seeking of God's heart and character to shift away from the belief that God purposefully placed this burden on us. It's going to take work to recognize the truth—that that's not how He operates. The first step, and perhaps the hardest one, is to try to walk out forgiveness toward the people who told you this falsehood. I know it's hard, but when I am faced with forgiveness that will not come easily, I envision Jesus on the cross crying out, "Father, forgive them for they know not what they do." He did this in the midst of being tortured, ridiculed, and killed. Holding on to your anger toward the people who instilled this deeply flawed concept within you is only hurting you. Instead of wasting any more emotional energy on them, use your time to invest in your own spiritual and mental health.

Potential Responses to Being Told That Depression Is a Punishment Sent by God:

Response #1: Depression is a legitimate, documented medical condition that afflicts an estimated 280 million people in the world without discrimination.[17] It can stem from trauma, biological factors, adverse life situations, or all of the above. Lamentations 3 makes it clear that God is not the author of our suffering.

Response #2: I do not serve an angry God who is waiting to punish me at any moment. Scripture tells me that He is a good father who desires to give good gifts to His children and that He does not willingly bring affliction on us. I serve a Savior whose story is founded in restoration, redemption, and the desire that none should perish. Your belief regarding God's character and heart toward me does not align with what I know about God through His Word.

False Belief #5: You Cannot Be Trusted with Responsibilities in Ministry

When someone is diagnosed with autism, the spectrum is so wide regarding their level of functioning that it would be highly unfair to make a snap judgment about their abilities without knowing them. The same is true regarding any mental health issues.

A person with mental health challenges can have struggles ranging from being highly anxious and unable to leave their home, to having intense but high-functioning anxiety; they might be unable to get out of bed due to a major depressive episode, or cope perfectly fine with their depression with the help of counseling, medication, or other measures. No matter where you fall on the grand spectrum of mental health diagnoses, when you want to serve God as much as the person next to you, it can hurt to be treated as if you are incapable of fulfilling your commitments or ministering to others.

The act of disqualifying fellow believers from church ministry is more than hurtful; it also keeps them from fulfilling God's charge to us in 1 Peter 4:10: "Each of you should use whatever gift you have received to serve others, as faithful stewards of God's grace in its various forms" (NIV). Operating in our unique giftings while living with the frailties that we *all* possess in some form allows

God to demonstrate that His power is made perfect in our weakness (2 Corinthians 12:9).

The opportunity to serve a higher purpose can truly keep some of us going on the most challenging of days. Not only does that act of service allow us to look past our pain and utilize our God-given gifts, but it also benefits the recipient and other believers who see us going through the same struggles they face. There is a reason peer support groups and mentorship programs are so successful. Knowing that someone is experiencing the same hardships, challenges, and diagnoses that you are is deeply comforting. Similarly, seeing that someone made it through everything you're currently battling provides great hope for the future.

A Moment for Mending

Has there been a ministry you wanted to get involved in but shied away from for fear of what others may say about you or think about you? Use the margin space on this page to list the benefits you would bring to your favorite ministry. Remember, any church would be lucky to have you come alongside them to serve. God has a ministry waiting for you that needs *you*—your heart, your talents, and your giftings.

Potential Responses to Being Told You're Not Trustworthy to Do Ministry:
Response #1: I feel called to serve in this area of ministry. My capabilities are not in any way handicapped by my struggles with anxiety or depression. I believe the challenges I have faced uniquely equip me with insight,

compassion, and a point of view that is desperately needed in the body of Christ.

Response #2: Not only am I highly capable of and responsible for doing ministry, but I am passionate about the volunteer work I do with (fill in the blank). I have no doubt I can complete my tasks effectively and to the glory of God.

False Belief #6: People with Mental Illness Are Demon-Possessed

I saved this one for last because I want to really spend some time unpacking this damaging misconception. I once spoke to a person with depression whose parents had the church try to perform an exorcism on her as a child. As you can imagine, this terrifying experience followed her into adulthood and lived on for many years in therapy. I sincerely hope that you've not had a similar experience.

Churches need to know it is *not biblical* to make a blanket judgment or statement when it comes to a Christian who is struggling with their mental health. There is not a single follower of God in the Bible who was demon-possessed. At best, the rationale that a believer can be possessed involves a preconceived belief based on personal feelings and assumptions rather than on any biblical foundation. Despite the attempt to change the terminology from demon-possessed to demonized, all the inferences remain that a believer can be under the influence and *authority* of demonic powers. Yet this is simply not true.

So, if a demon cannot inhabit a Christian, what does scripture have to say about Satan's influence when it comes to believers? The Bible is clear that Satan schemes against Christians (Ephesians 6:11). We know that the enemy is on the prowl, seeking to destroy believers (1 Peter 5:8). We see in Luke 4:2 how Satan and his demonic influence sought to tempt Jesus and attacked Him in the areas where it was assumed Jesus would be most vulnerable.

While we obviously don't want to be unaware there's an enemy of our souls that we must stand guard against, we also don't need to live in fear that there's a demon around every corner, waiting and able to inhabit our being. Making blanket statements that people with depression, anxiety, and other mental health conditions are demon-possessed is not only harmful to those already vulnerable and hurting, but it's also categorically untrue.

When we accept Christ as our Savior, He tells us He will send a helper, the Holy Spirit, to live within us. Let's look at a few scriptures that drive this point home:

> If you love me, you will keep my commandments.
> And I will ask the Father, and he will give you
> another Helper, to be with you forever, even the
> Spirit of truth, whom the world cannot receive,
> because it neither sees him nor knows him. You
> know him, for he dwells with you and will be in you.
> (John 14:15-17)

> What harmony can there be between Christ and
> Satan?
> (2 Corinthians 6:15 TPT)

> Do you not know that you are God's temple and that
> God's Spirit dwells in you? . . . God's temple is holy,
> and you are that temple.
> (1 Corinthians 3:16-17)

The one who is in you is greater than the one who is
in the world.

(1 John 4:4 NIV)

Would the Holy Spirit really allow an evil spirit to dwell
inside the same body as Himself? No, of course not. You
are God's holy temple, and He is a jealous God. Simply
put, the Holy Spirit is *not* going to share His space.
Temptation, spiritual oppression, and spiritual warfare
exist, but if you have a relationship with Jesus, there is no
demonic possession.

A Moment for Mending

Being told or treated as if you harbored evil spirits
is so damaging and so wrong. I want you to go to
the scriptural affirmations in the back of this book
as many times as you need to and speak out the
truth about Who you belong to, Who dwells within
you, and the identity you have forever in Christ.
You are held in the palm of His hand.

*Potential Responses to Being Told That Christians Can
Be Demon-Possessed*

Response #1: I am sorry to hear that you share a belief
that has been damaging to so many in the mental health
community. Sadly, this false belief is the reason so many
believers have been driven away from church. I could not
disagree further, but I would be happy to give you some
resources to read that offer a biblical perspective.

Response #2: Romans 8:9-11 shares that the Spirit of
God dwells inside of me, and 1 John 4:4 tells us that He

who is in us is greater than he who is in the world. In other words, my God doesn't share His space. There is no Airbnb for demonic rental here, only a temple of the Holy Spirit.

Sadly, there will always be myths about mental health amongst Christians and non-Christians alike, but that is why ongoing conversation about this topic is so important. To change this stigma that's kept so many believers suffering in silence, the church needs people with the courage to stand up and say, "Actually, that's not true," when it comes to lies surrounding the topic of mental health. We need to see a Christian equivalent to the #MeToo movement, where we can freely and without shame share that we, too, have struggled—and do struggle—with our mental health, and it in no way diminishes our strength, value, or spirituality. Simply by bringing our stories into the light, you and I can be part of the solution.

Jesus and Therapy

Jesus

If reengaging in the church or a relationship with Jesus has felt too triggering, you can still ask God to reveal if other unbiblical points of view have taken root in your faith. If you have fallen prey to the lie that His grace was for everyone but you, that your battle with mental health was a punishment, or that you were unworthy to serve because of your struggles, ask the Lord to transform those wounds by His radical grace—freely available to you.

Therapy

Is there a particular mental health "myth" that has resonated with you? Or an experience similar to one of my own that reading this book has brought to the surface? Don't bury it. Talk to your therapist and get the support you deserve as you bring it into the light and discuss the old memories, beliefs, or experiences that have resurfaced, along with any upsetting effect they might have on you. The only way out is through, my friend.

Seven

Healing Takes Time

The Only Way Out Is Through

"Healing doesn't mean the damage never existed.
It means the damage no longer controls your life."

—AKSHAY DUBEY, MOTIVATIONAL SPEAKER

Trigger Warning: The author discusses being committed to the psychiatric hospital in this chapter.

While I'd love to tell you that all my mental health issues cleared up during those first six months in counseling, nothing could be further from the truth. I was still suicidal, cutting myself and drowning in depression, thanks to the constant presence of my abusers both in my home and at church. Therapy offered a safe place temporarily, but it couldn't fix the life waiting for me outside the therapist's door. And until I was old enough to advocate for myself, escape my childhood church, and create boundaries surrounding how I was treated, all I could do in the short term was cope.

Throughout this time, I continued to go to counseling weekly. However, as time passed, Dr. G began to realize there was likely a bigger barrier hindering my healing, but as to what it was, he wasn't sure. Unable to get the necessary answers from me, he asked my mom if there were any other traumatic events in my past that I may have blocked out. She conveyed to him the extent of my childhood abuse, much of which I had repressed the memories of or was too young to recall clearly. When Dr. G sat me down to share the details of the physical abuse I'd endured as an infant and young child at my father's hand, every ounce of color left my face. In shock and enraged, I stormed out of that counseling session shaking like a leaf but intent on getting an explanation straight from the abuser's mouth.

Corner a narcissist about the abuse they have spent years denying, and watch the fireworks begin! When I told my dad what my therapist had relayed, he immediately became furious and started telling me that my mom was lying and my counselor was planting false memories in my brain. As Dad went on and on, I felt more and more sick to my stomach.

"Tabitha, that happened to your brother, not you!" he finally said.

Ahh . . . there was the admission of abuse. My dad's denials quite literally made me sick. I spent that entire weekend vomiting and lying on the bathroom floor. For the next two months, I was in and out of the hospital and on leave from work. My physical health had finally caught up to my mental health, which had never been worse. My entire system was beginning to crash and burn.

Broken in mind, body, and spirit, I'd rejected my faith entirely by this point. I could not love a God who seemed to "hate" me, as the church elders had claimed. I couldn't follow someone who would lead me down the paths I'd been forced to walk. I couldn't believe in someone who would allow me to endure all this pain. For the first time in my life, I refused to pray or to be scared into following Jesus anymore. All my life, my walk with God had been fear-based, and now I made a promise to myself that I would never come back to my faith out of being afraid, bullied, or guilted into following Him. No more.

Growing up in the church, I had met every type of Christian imaginable. And almost every encounter made me ashamed to call myself a Christ follower. Thanks to those experiences, I was convinced the church was not the place I could go to be authentic, nor was it a safe space for my pain. And Christians? The world loved me better than they did. Their love looked nothing like Jesus. Sadly, the very people "doing God's work" were the tipping point for me to abandon the only belief system I'd ever known in hopes of finding something and someone real.

Rock Bottom in 3, 2, 1 . . .

If you had asked me just a few months earlier to identify what my rock bottom was, I likely would have pointed to my suicide attempts. I had no idea at the time that rock bottom was yet to come.

On top of seeing him weekly, Dr. G suggested that it would be beneficial for me to see a psychiatrist as well, since my depression was not resolving itself. This was around the time when my mandatory summer trip to see my dad was coming up again. I *knew* I wouldn't get through one more visit with him, and I didn't plan to.

So I created a detailed suicide plan that I would wait to carry out until after I'd arrived at my dad's Midwest home. My father had scoffed at my prior suicide attempt and said I only did it for attention. Then, knowing I was in the depths of my depression, he'd told me no one liked people like me who were never happy, so I may as well kill myself.

I'll show him, I thought. Maybe finding my dead body would finally make him feel sorry. Or maybe he'd step right over my body and carry on with his stubborn denial of any wrongdoing. Just days before my siblings and I were to board the plane for our summer trip, I finished my goodbye letters. In a matter of days, I'd set my plan into motion.

Then, at the beginning of May, I went to an appointment with a female psychiatrist I'd never met before. I was tired, so tired. Maybe I just wanted someone to save me; I don't know. But when she asked me if I felt safe, instead of lying to her so I could go through with my plan to end my life, I said, "No."

"When you leave my office, can you promise me that you won't try to hurt yourself again?" she asked.

Again, I said, "No."

"Would you feel safer if you could go somewhere where they would watch you and take care of you, where you can receive some extra counseling?" she pressed.

Her offer seemed so inviting, like a little break from the never-ending stress in my life. Who wouldn't want a little extra support and protection? It sounded almost like a retreat in my mind—OK, sign me up!

The "somewhere" the psychiatrist was offering wasn't the retreat I'd envisioned, however—it was the local psych ward. I hadn't the slightest idea of what being admitted to a psychiatric hospital would look like, but within a matter of hours, I had been strip-searched for drugs and weapons in the women's bathroom while being treated more like an inmate than a mentally ill teen.

Ahh . . . rock bottom . . . *there you are.*

While my time in the psych ward was the absolute lowest moment in my life, little did I know it would set me on a course of pursuing deep emotional healing that would last a lifetime and eventually transform me into the woman I am today—a little at a time.

Healing Is Hard

Healing is hard, sacred work that's not instantaneous, easy, or automatically granted to those following Jesus. Life will leave its share of scars, and sometimes we go through incredibly challenging and traumatic experiences that forever alter us. But our response to those traumas isn't written in the stars or etched in stone. We may not have had a choice regarding the pain inflicted on us, but we *can* fight to not let it dictate the rest of our lives. Sometimes, the decision to finally face our "demons," whatever they may be, comes after countless years of the same triggers, the same trauma responses, the same cyclical processes. Finally, one day we realize we cannot possibly stay in this space any longer and would rather tackle the pain head-on than try to run away from it anymore. And often, that choice to go toe-to-toe with our past has to be made again and again. But that courageous decision to get to the root of your trauma and wounding is the place from which true growth and long-term healing can spring forth.

And long-term healing takes a long time. I'm still on that journey. For example, in my early thirties, I hit a wall in that never-ending healing journey. I was sick of my old ways of coping and my lack of healthy boundaries in relationships, and I knew I needed to change. Having been in and out of therapy for over fifteen years, I'd healed from so much—but there was still more work to be done.

101

Becoming a spouse and a parent brought things to light that needed to be addressed in therapy. All those old ways of thinking were still my primary operating system. And those coping mechanisms I'd developed early on were proving destructive to me and my family. Suddenly, I could see all the things I didn't want to pass on to my own children. And let me just tell you: being a generational curse breaker is no small feat. Carving out a healthy path when all you know is what *not* to do is challenging, to say the least.

If you've ever spoken to anyone who is on an intensive healing journey, they will tell you that at first, healing feels like breaking. You're losing the only version of yourself you've ever known. You're uprooting your core thoughts and belief systems. You're losing people or choosing to walk away from the ones who are keeping you sick or finding yourself stuck in unhealthy cycles or situations. You're coming face-to-face with the memories you've buried, the pain you've run from, and the wounds that previously informed your identity. I often describe my adult healing process as a free fall. It was as if someone had enrolled me in some crazy trust exercise, and I wasn't sure when—or where—I would land, if my feet would find solid ground, or who would still be there when all was said and done.

To be clear, I don't wish to discourage anyone from continuing their healing process. What I want is for you to know you're not alone on the days when it feels like you're breaking into a million pieces, when you question if you'll ever be whole again, or when you wonder if you'll ever be capable of living a life not dictated by your wounds. I know how it feels to anxiously await a time when there are no more layers to peel back, not knowing if that time will ever come. But on the days when you want to throw in the towel, I want you to remember something: you're fighting not just for yourself and the peace you deserve, but for the generations coming after you who will receive the gift of a different story because of the work you are putting in right now to change your family history. What you're doing is powerful and paramount.

It's going to be worth it, and you're going to be proud of yourself. Just give yourself grace when you feel like your recovery is one step forward, two steps back. It's OK and necessary to rest because this process is a marathon, not a sprint. The key is not to quit. The goal is to keep showing up for yourself.

Therapy Now

For many, healing is a lifelong pursuit. Following the birth of my third and last child, I fully immersed myself in the deep work of healing my inner child and revisiting all the things I'd buried, avoided, and convinced myself no longer had an impact on me. I committed to showing up for therapy sessions until I became the adult I'd needed as a child. I was determined to be the parent my children deserved and a woman I could be proud of.

The two types of therapy that have been the most transformative for me personally have been cognitive behavioral therapy (CBT) and eye movement desensitization and reprocessing (EMDR).

Cognitive behavioral therapy is a short-term form of behavioral treatment. It helps people problem-solve. CBT also reveals the relationship between beliefs, thoughts, and feelings and the behaviors that follow. Through CBT, people learn that their perceptions directly influence how they respond to specific situations. In other words, a person's thought process informs their behaviors and actions.[18]

Eye movement desensitization and reprocessing is a psychotherapy treatment originally designed to alleviate the distress associated with traumatic memories. EMDR therapy facilitates accessing the traumatic memory network so that information processing is enhanced, with new associations forged between the traumatic memory and more adaptive memories or information. These new associations are thought to result in complete information processing, new learning, elimination of emotional distress, and development of cognitive insights.[19]

During the most significant period of healing in my adult life, I spent over five years frequently attending EMDR sessions. This is where my hardest moments of abuse and trauma were reprocessed. I think most individuals who incorporate EMDR in their recovery journey will tell you they have a love-hate relationship with it. It brought me face-to-face with some of the most eye-opening, lightbulb-coming-on, "this changes everything" realizations about my past and myself. While these sessions brought immense truth and peace into my life, I had to fight hell itself and work harder than I'd ever had to in order to achieve that peace.

What the Bible Says about Counseling

As counseling became more and more instrumental in my life, I wanted to know what the Bible had to say about it. Were there any references to be found, other than Isaiah 9:6, where Jesus is referred to as the Wonderful Counselor? Upon digging further, I discovered that the word "counsel" is found 133 times throughout Scripture.

There are three Hebrew words that translate to *counsel* in the Bible: *parakletos*, *symboulous*, and *yoez*. The sum of their definitions is to advise, resolve, guide, plan, consult, or instruct. Let's dive into a few of those verses that reference the wisdom to be found in receiving counsel:

> Personally, I am convinced about you, my brothers and sisters, that you yourselves are full of goodness, amply filled with all [spiritual] knowledge, and competent to admonish and counsel and instruct one another.
> (Romans 15:14 AMP)

> Without consultation and wise advice, plans are frustrated, but with many counselors they are established and succeed.
> (Proverbs 15:22 AMP)

> A wise man listens to advice.
> (Proverbs 12:15)

> Where there is no [wise, intelligent] guidance, the people fall [and go off course like a ship without a helm],
> But in the abundance of [wise and godly] counselors there is victory.
> (Proverbs 11:14 AMP)

> Getting wisdom is the most important thing you can do! And with your wisdom, develop common sense and good judgment.
> (Proverbs 4:7 TLB)

> Use all wisdom to teach and counsel each other.
> (Colossians 3:16 ERV)

You will keep on guiding me all my life with your
wisdom and counsel.

(Psalm 73:24 TLB)

In His Word, God demonstrates that receiving advice, guidance, and counsel is admirable, recommended, and beneficial. God is always working, and often He uses people to accomplish His purposes on earth. As in my case, and perhaps yours, the trained professionals who have invested their time and expertise to partner with me on my mental health journey are the wise counsel that God suggested we seek out and utilize.

I hope the realization that you're not alone on the road to healing, the validation that healing really is *that* hard sometimes, and the knowledge that receiving counsel is encouraged in scripture will uplift your spirit and give you the nudge you need to keep fighting for your emotional well-being. I encourage you to give yourself grace the next time something you thought you'd already dealt with rears its ugly head. Because healing takes time. Know that simply by continuing to show up and face the hard things as they arise, you are creating a transformation in your family that will last for generations to come.

Jesus and Therapy

Jesus

How has God provided helpers for you as you've navigated your mental health struggles? Have you come to know Him as the Wonderful Counselor scripture speaks of? God has provided a comforter, the Holy Spirit, to always be with us. He has given us the gift of seeking out caring, competent professionals to compassionately guide us through whatever processing, growth, and healing needs to take place. If we look closely, we can see His hand in everything and take joy in the assurance that He advocates for His people to receive wise counsel—and know that He loves us, cares about us, and is pleased with us.

Therapy

With your therapist, evaluate any frustration you may be feeling with your healing journey, the length of time it's taking, or the exasperation you feel when uncovering new issues or triggers. Often, it's hard to see how much we've grown during our time in treatment. So it can be encouraging to hear a counselor share some of the changes they've observed, whether healthy boundaries they've watched us set or the way they've noticed that our reactions to painful triggers have shifted over time. Sometimes, that simple acknowledgment and applause is enough to keep us from giving up when the going gets tough.

Eight

Rock Bottom

Facing Brokenness and Setting Boundaries

"I have learned to kiss the waves that throw me up
against the Rock of Ages."

—COMMONLY ATTRIBUTED TO CHARLES H. SPURGEON

Trigger Warning: This chapter talks about suicide, self-harm, and a psychiatric hospital stay.

It took all of half a day in the psychiatric hospital for me to realize I'd made a colossal mistake. The staff was unbearably cold and treated me like a criminal instead of someone who had voluntarily checked herself in. At least, I thought the decision had been a voluntary one. I quickly discovered that the paperwork filed by the psychiatrist stated that the court had ordered me to stay inpatient, so I couldn't check myself out or leave until the staff deemed I was ready to handle life on the outside. In other words, I was a prisoner and this was no retreat.

The hospital's walls were filled with unspeakable sentiments from the patients about the staff members who worked there. After only a day there, I was inclined to agree with the scribblings penned all around me. Hardened by their environment, the staff lacked the slightest bit of compassion. Sickened at the callousness they showed toward the patients in their care, I quickly came to the disappointing realization that I had no value as a human being in their eyes. I was just another number in their charge.

I spent my entire first day in the psych ward sitting in the common area, listening to the ramblings of a schizophrenic girl who wouldn't stop talking about how she'd stabbed her mom and little brother. Though I was a little bit afraid of her, I reasoned she would be in juvenile detention instead of the psychiatric hospital if she really had done that, *right?*

I still recall my first night there a little too vividly, like something out of a horror movie. My room, like the others, was sterile. All the furniture had rounded corners, there were no curtains on the windows, (for obvious reasons), and each patient received one small, itchy blanket. Naturally, there were no locks on the inside of the doors, but there were locks on the outside. So they could lock me in, but if a violent patient escaped, there'd be no keeping them out of my room. No, people with mental health struggles are not inherently more prone to violence, but I was a frightened kid with Suzy-Stabs-A-Lot just a few doors down, so logic gave way to fear once the sun set.

It was so cold, and I never felt so much like the child I was until I lay awake shivering and alone in the middle of the night, listening to people scream and talk to themselves down the hall. That night I cried and cried and vowed I would do whatever it took to get out of there. I had never been so lonely or terrified in my entire life. My heart physically ached at the thought of being left in that hellhole with no one to save me, no one to hold me, and no one to protect me. It was the absolute lowest moment of my life.

The next morning, my new routine began. Morning and night, I'd line up to take whatever new cocktail of meds they were trying on me that week. I dutifully participated in all that was expected of me each day, but I always dreaded the coming of nightfall. The darkness felt even darker there, and the nights were like a bad dream I couldn't wake from.

In no time at all, thanks to my astute powers of observation, I figured out the key to getting released from the psych ward. First, I had to attend every possible counseling appointment and group session. Second, I just needed to lie my butt off and vow that I'd never hurt myself again. If I played my cards right, they'd eventually believe me.

Hail Mary

After running from God, denying, cursing, and turning my back on Him, I was literally and figuratively trapped. The only thing I knew to do as I was panicking on my first night in the facility was cry out to Jesus. But I didn't want the Jesus my church had shown me; I needed to find the One who was good and wouldn't leave me alone in that bitter, cold room. Tired of living under a cloud of condemnation, I needed a God who had enough grace to cover all my mistakes. But could God really love a broken, depressed, sobbing mess of a girl locked up in the psych ward?

Just as I was searching for the right words to pray, I remembered the promise I had made myself when I walked away from my faith—I'd never again let fear be the reason I came to Jesus. But there I was, more scared than I'd ever been in my entire life, and I thought, *This can't be how it happens.* I wanted it to be His kindness that drew me in. If I was going to approach Jesus, my decision needed to be more than a Hail Mary in a time of desperation.

So, instead of throwing myself on God's mercy, my stubborn and petrified teenage self paged the staff to beg for another blanket. After they begrudgingly brought one to my frigid room, I curled up and made my body as small as it could get and, once again, cried myself to sleep.

To the observing eye, I had been all but abandoned in that psychiatric ward. Later in life, some would even scoff, "Where was your God then?" But you know what I see when I close my eyes and relive that moment? I see the Lord holding me, stroking my hair, and wiping my tears. I see Him refusing to let me go, no matter how hard I pushed Him away. I can't recount that memory without the absolute assurance He was carrying me even then.

Sure, I may have been saying and doing all the wrong things in those days, but God's love for me was relentless. He pursued me even in the darkest nights, melting my anger a little at a time. He met me in my pain and beckoned me to come, broken as I was. While still confused about where I stood with Jesus and what I knew about Him, within the walls of that psych ward I was beginning to realize that, just maybe, everything I'd been taught about Him in my childhood church was wrong.

Maybe, just maybe, I didn't have to hold myself back from Jesus because I was too broken for Him to love. Maybe He wasn't ashamed of me. Maybe His grace was enough for me. Maybe His unmerited favor was there all along.

What if He loved me the way a parent is supposed to love their child—without condition and without measure, simply because I'm theirs? What if His heart hurt just as much as mine did over what His "followers" had said and done to me? What would happen if I stopped running from the only One who offered me a love I didn't have to earn?

My Fading Religious Façade

Prior to my experience in the psych ward, I had spent months in and out of the hospital due to failing physical health, days of overmedicating just to stay numb, and nights of cursing God and my very existence. I wanted to hate God for the life I believed He'd "sentenced" me to. Quite frankly, hating Him required far less energy than the time, healing, and counseling it ultimately took to strip away all my false beliefs and put my faith in Jesus. Hating God was certainly easier than all the courage it took to let the only foundation I'd known crumble around me. I let it crumble when I finally realized that Jesus had been nailed to that cross to save me from the whitewashed religious façade of the life I had been living.

I knew religion like the back of my hand, and I didn't want to suffocate under the weight of a legalistic existence anymore. However, I could never seem to outrun the pull I felt on my soul. Something in those depths hoped there was something—or someone—better. *If* I were going to come back to faith, that faith was going to look different. It had to. People were going to be drawn to Jesus through me, not turned away.

I had no idea the purpose He had in store for me, and though it would take me many years down a long and winding road to find my way back, His plan for my redemption was already in action. God would use my story to make Himself known, but first He had to make His true self known to me.

Escaping My Glass Cage

Due to my past plans and attempts, and constant suicidal ideation, I was on suicide watch throughout the duration of my stay in the psychiatric hospital. This meant whether I was in the bathroom, sleeping, or eating, I had to be checked on every fifteen minutes to ensure I was alive and unharmed.

As the days began to blur together, I lost count of how many therapy sessions I'd attended with the hospital's psychiatrist. Despite the endless meetings, the depression was still all-consuming, and I was starting to feel at a total loss for how to get myself released. I wanted to be treated like a person again. I wanted the staff to know I was funny, intelligent, clever, sweet, and kind. The depression wasn't all I was, and I was tired of being treated like a walking diagnosis. I wanted my own bed in my own room. Even as I questioned if I'd ever feel OK again, I knew the answers wouldn't be found in that dark place. I just wanted to go home.

I felt as if I were in an uncomfortable glass cage, and my desperation to escape increasingly consumed my thoughts. Just as I was at the point of contemplating a prison break, the staff allowed me to have an outing with my mom to the mall. My first taste of freedom in a week was to Payless, the only shoe store in Hawaii that stocked my big ol' shoe size. I tried to enjoy the evening, but as I observed everyone my age laughing, shopping, and living in the moment, all I could think about was the perdition that awaited me.

When the time came to head back to the facility, I lost it. Huddled against the passenger door, having the mother of all panic attacks, I sobbed and begged my mom not to take me back to the psychiatric ward. "Just take me home, Mom!" I begged her. "We can leave all my belongings there. They can burn them for all I care. Just please don't make me go back!"

As my mom explained why she couldn't take me home, something in me started to shut down. It was as if my body knew I'd have to stop feeling anything to survive walking back into that building. I felt an emotional sort of death as I resigned myself to what I must do.

Since I'd been off the premises, I was subjected to the joy of being searched in the bathroom again, which somehow felt even more violating than it had the first time. The only thing I *would have* smuggled in was an Orange Julius, but I knew better than to do anything that might jeopardize my release. That night I sat in the communal area for a few minutes before bed, long enough to watch an ambulance pull up and admit a young girl around my age. She had just overdosed, had her stomach pumped, and then was promptly dumped at the entrance to this hellhole. As I wished for her sake that she could recover anywhere else, my thoughts were interrupted by the mandatory call for bedtime. Too tired and numb to cry myself to sleep, I lay in silence until a fitful sleep overtook me.

Outside of the long nights left alone with my thoughts, my days as an inpatient are largely a blur. Finally, they came to an end.

However, I do remember my last day there. As I signed my release papers, my therapist told me that I had a lot of potential. "I hope you do something great with your life," I was told. "If you can just make it long enough to see what your future holds, I know you will accomplish anything you set your mind to."

Once I was officially discharged, I was so relieved to walk through the hospital's double doors and feel the sun on my face that I could have kissed the grass. I was *finally* free. Although I wish I had kinder things to say about the state of this particular mental health facility, in retrospect, there's only one thing I feel like I gained through my psychiatric stay: insight. I'd witnessed firsthand how untreated psychiatric disorders can destroy a person's life and how deeply unresolved trauma affects our mental health.

Promises

On that long drive home, with my mom behind the steering wheel, I did a lot of contemplating. What did I need to do differently to not end up in that hellhole again? Since I was still a minor, would I even be *allowed* to say no to my guardians or create boundaries to protect myself? I didn't choose the background I came from, and the abuse and circumstances driving my depression certainly weren't my fault. Somehow, sitting in that passenger seat, I knew it was time for me to take responsibility for who I'd one day become. At just sixteen, that seemingly small act of ownership propelled me into a lifelong pursuit of growth and healing. I wasn't going to let my broken past dictate my future.

So many things needed to change; yet, first, I knew I needed to make my way to Jesus. If that meant fighting my way through the crowd (other Christians) and jumping over all the hurdles that had kept me from Him (false beliefs perpetuated by His followers and my own family), so be it. I had tried this world without Jesus. I had tried to numb the pain any way I could. I'd put myself in harm's way again and again, trying to escape all the hurt. I'd run until I couldn't run anymore. The only way to get better was to face everything I'd been trying to bury. But there was no way to face the past without Him, and what's more, I no longer wanted to.

I was admittedly a bit rusty at praying, but as we continued to travel down the highway, I was ready to lay all my burdens down and fall at His feet. My halted prayer went something like this: *God, I don't know if You're there, and I don't know if You're listening to me anymore. I don't really know anything anymore, and I'm not making any promises, but I want to try to find my way to You. If You're real, like I think You are, please help me.*

I had waited until His kindness drew me in and I no longer wanted to deny Him. I wanted to discover who God really was and how much He loved me. And as I uttered my prayer on the way home from the psychiatric facility, we came up a hill and, to my disbelief, just on the other side of it there was a rainbow. I had made no promises that day, but clearly He had.

A Firm Foundation

I knew that I'd built my entire foundation on false beliefs about Jesus and myself. But even with that revelation, I didn't know what to believe instead. No one was magically waiting on my doorstep when we got home from the psych ward to help me process my extensive trauma and reframe my entire belief system. Instead, the days and years that followed would be filled with the daunting task of dismantling nearly two decades of lies, little by little. The hard work of healing meant rebuilding brick by brick with the help of Jesus and my therapist.

As I settled back into my old life, it was clearer than ever that I needed a game plan if I wanted to have the slightest chance of becoming healthy. First, I'd have to remove myself from a lot of the situations I'd been in and set boundaries in many of my relationships. Then I'd have to survey and address the damage. From that point forward, it would be me and my Savior against the world.

Lord, please let what little fight I have left in me be enough for me to build a different life, I prayed.

Over the next few chapters, we're going to work through some of the most important lessons I had to learn during my lifelong pursuit of healing. Specifically, I needed to learn how to:

- Quit believing I was a burden
- Stop chasing perfection and start accepting that God's grace was for me
- Shift my thinking from believing I only had a testimony once I was on the other side of the fire to realizing I already had an effective testimony that I could share with others
- Understand that God uses broken people to accomplish His purposes
- Walk through a lifetime of church hurt and come out on the other side being able to attend and participate in the body of Christ without always feeling triggered

While no two experiences are alike, if you can relate on any level to the feelings discussed in these eight chapters; if you've ever felt trapped by pain you should have been protected from; if you've ever felt unworthy of being rescued and eventually believed you deserved nothing more than all the wounding being inflicted on you; if you've ever felt alone, exposed to the elements without an umbrella, like the only person who had your back was you—I need to tell you something.

You aren't irreparably broken, even if you were treated as such. You weren't sheltered then but come join me now under the shadow of God's wings and protection. You're safe now. You still have the power to move forward and become everything God meant for you to be before people hurt you. You're not ruined. You're not damaged goods. You're rebuilding. You're healing, and the people who hurt you don't get the final word in your story. Jesus does, and He already spoke victory over you: "For everyone born of God is victorious and overcomes the world; and this is the victory that has conquered and overcome the world—our [continuing, persistent] faith [in Jesus the Son of God]" (1 John 5:4 AMP). And so, my friend, this is not where your story ends.

Jesus and Therapy

Jesus

Have you resisted a relationship with Jesus because people in religious circles led you to believe that Jesus would never want you? Did all the rules and restrictions placed on your external behavior lead you to believe it was impossible to please Him? Ask God to illuminate the people and moments that were the straws that broke the camel's back and led you to walk away. Write them down and hold on to this list until we revisit it in the final chapter.

Therapy

Can you identify your rock-bottom moment? Unpack this experience with your counselor. What led you to the breaking point? How did you feel when you sank to the lowest depth? Are you still there today? Walk through the emotions with the help of your therapist. We can't heal from what we won't face.

Nine

You Aren't a Burden

Reestablishing Your Identity and Worth

> The fact that you're struggling
> doesn't make you a burden.
> It doesn't make you unlovable or
> undesirable or undeserving of care.
> It doesn't make you too much
> or too sensitive or too needy.
> It makes you human.
>
> —DANIELL KOEPKE, *DARING TO TAKE UP SPACE*

Trigger Warning: The author discusses suicide in this chapter.

Against my better judgment, when I was almost eighteen years old, I packed up to go live with my father in the Midwest so I could attend college at the university where he was a professor. My brother was already living with my dad and had completed a couple of years of schooling at the same college. Though I didn't want to live with my dad and knew it was the worst possible thing for my mental health, it was the only way I could see myself affording to go to school. For the past couple of years, I'd been working fifty to seventy hours a week to cover my expenses through my high school years. I did my best to pay for anything I needed—my first car, my clothing, my spending money—as well as helping my mom however I could.

My plan came to a devastating halt right before Christmas. I received a detailed letter from my father telling me that I couldn't come live with him, that he couldn't give me any support to attend college. In fact, he didn't want to talk to me at all. He said he needed a "break" from me. That I was "too much." That his life was easier without me in it.

While I can see in hindsight that this absolutely worked out for my good, there's nothing quite like being told straight up that someone needs a break from you, to have your own family perpetuate the fear that you're hard to love. The break my dad demanded ended up being permanent, and I've been estranged from him ever since. Thanks to his actions, it's taken most of my adult life to feel wanted and to understand that not everyone's humoring me until someone better comes along.

My dad's rejection led me to proactively withdraw from people I cared about in a misguided attempt to prevent them from inevitably getting sick of me. I needed to save myself from the pain of rejection and to save them from the burden of being my friend, didn't I?

Self-Isolation Strikes Again

If you took a poll of all the people in the world who struggle with a mental health disorder and asked them for one of their primary concerns, they would likely mention the fear of being a burden to their loved ones.

By definition, feeling like a burden means believing your life or situation brings trouble to those around you or oppresses them, or that others simply bear with you out of obligation. Whether you feel you're already a weight to those around you or you constantly fear becoming one, it can be all-consuming.

Perhaps you're worried that your depression is becoming too heavy for some people. Or maybe you can't bear to tell your family that you are having another bad day. Surely your friends will become sick of your struggles, right? Wouldn't it just be easier to self-isolate? Wouldn't that be the kindest thing for those around you?

I get it. I've been there. In the moment, each of those justifications for self-isolating sounds entirely convincing and nothing like the blatant, dangerous lie that it is. Feeling like a burden and a drain on family and friends is also one of the most tragic motivators behind suicide attempts. Depression is often the motivating factor behind comments like, "You're finally free to go live your life," or "You don't have to worry about me now," or "I won't hold you back anymore."

If you've dealt with depression, anxiety, OCD, PTSD, or some other psychiatric condition, you've probably found yourself wrestling with a similar lie: that life would be easier for everyone else if you weren't in the picture. I've been on both sides of the fence: times when I feel like the drain on the relationship, and times when I'm the one offering a lifeline to someone who wants to die. If you've been a support system in such a high-stakes situation, you know it's no bed of roses, but you also know that when your friend or family member makes it through that darkness, that it's worth every second it cost you.

In this chapter, we're going to talk about why you matter, the ways in which you are so much more than your diagnosis, how you can build a "mental health first aid kit," the process for developing an amazing support network, the best methods for incorporating self-soothing skills into your routine, and so much more!

Why You Matter

Not long ago, the stories of two heartbreaking suicides came across my desk. Their similarities immediately struck me: both tragic events took place late at night, and both happened while the individuals were isolated and alone. While these individuals could have been smiling and laughing hours earlier, once they were alone with their thoughts, the darkness took over.

Before we go any further on this topic of suicide, I want to tell you something. If you're struggling with suicidal ideation, your loved ones would much, much rather you wake them up out of a dead sleep than have you decide not to "bother" them ever again with one tragic, irreversible decision. Please do not give up and think you are doing your family and friends a favor. They need you just as much as you need them; you just can't see it right now. Regardless of the day or time, reach out as many times as it takes.

I've sat up till 3:00 a.m. with suicidal loved ones who were scared to be alone. I've hidden the kitchen knives to remove the temptation. I've called and set up the appointments and helped search for just the right psychiatrist. I've stepped in as many times as needed to pull my loved ones back from the ledge. I share this to emphasize that when someone loves you, they aren't going to give up on you. When someone chooses you, they get all of you.

Will there be hard times and moments when your support system needs to rotate and take breaks? Absolutely! But your support system is there because your life is precious to them and *they can't imagine a world without you in it.*

Some Only Stay for a Season

Because I've been the one needing help in some seasons of my life while at other times the one offering the help, I've learned not to take it personally when a friend or family member is unable to be emotionally available. We all have seasons when we are so wrapped up in what we're going through that we need to pull back from people in order to preserve our own emotional energy.

I've come to believe that the people who come and go don't deserve to be vilified. That's because if I've learned anything after reflecting on my twenty-five-plus years of living with anxiety and depression, it's that God sends some people for just a season, even when you most desire one person who will stay with you through it all.

It took time, but as I healed, I slowly realized that not everyone was equipped to walk this path with me for a lifetime. Did this feel triggering and play into the narrative I already had in my head that I was a burden? You know it did! But after decades of fighting for people to stay with me and love me, I finally reached a place where I could look back and see those relationships as the lifeline they were for that specific season. For those God-ordained moments in time, those people were Jesus in the flesh to me, tangibly demonstrating His love. Some of my most vulnerable and life-changing moments were with people who are no longer in my day-to-day life.

And so I have learned to lovingly receive the people in my season, learn the lessons I can learn from them, and then gracefully let them go when the time comes that we are no longer walking the same path or going in the same direction.

You Aren't Your Diagnosis

Another one of the things I had to learn to let go of in my thirties was the act of warring against my diagnosis. I have wasted far too many years fighting against a part of me that is just that—a small part. You aren't only your diagnosis. You are so much more. The people in your life get to benefit from all the beauty found within you—your unique points of view, sense of humor, creativity, hobbies, passion, and friendship.

Let's take a moment to make a list. You can use the space on the next page or your favorite notebook or journal. At the top of the page, write "My Diagnosis" on one side and "My Whole Self" on the other. Now, draw a line down the middle, and under "My Diagnosis," list out whatever is relevant to you: bipolar, ADHD, anxiety, PTSD, and so on. Then, under "My Whole Self," jot down what makes you unique: your personality and character traits, the hobbies you enjoy, your goals, the wisdom you've gleaned through life, etc. If you're struggling to find the good right now, perhaps ask a loved one or two to name their favorite thing about you. Feel free to grab a pen and use the prompts below as a jumping-off point to help you recognize all the value you hold in this life.

My Diagnosis	My Whole Self

Writing Prompts:

My friends can always count
on me to be _____.
                    (loving/loyal/funny/etc.)

I am my best self
when I'm _____.
      (with friends/in nature/reading a good book/etc.)

I love to laugh at _____.

My heart aches to see _____ change.

The world needs my _____.
           (sense of humor/insight/talent/etc.)

My unique gifts are _____.

People say I'm good at _____.
            (drawing/cooking/crafting/etc.)

My greatest strength is _____.

Four Essentials for Maintaining Your Mental Health

After living with my diagnoses for so many years, I eventually got to the point where I could feel my depression or anxiety building like a wave coming toward me, pulling me in like the tide into choppy waters. And now I know when I'm about to be pulled under. At times, this was brought on by periods of prolonged stress; other times it came with the territory when facing relational challenges, financial pressure, or parental hardships. Eventually, when I knew I was about to enter a sink-or-swim season of life, I learned how to prepare for the best possible outcome. Sometimes feeling equipped and empowered meant removing a commitment or external stressor, telling a friend or family member that I felt a rough patch coming on, scheduling extra counseling sessions, or getting a prescription filled.

I've found four essentials that are key to maintaining my mental health:

1. Create a mental health first aid kit.

Just as we all have a first aid kit in case of emergencies at home for physical injuries, we can prepare a mental health first aid kit of sorts for those rough patches. Every kit will look different because we're all unique. Yours could contain resources like phone numbers, deep breathing techniques, encouraging podcasts, and even specific medication. For example, my kit contains items that help me quickly self-soothe: a journal, my Bible, a weighted lap blanket, a sound machine, candles, Epsom salts, lavender essential oil, an abundant supply of chocolate, all ten seasons of *Friends* on Netflix, and gift cards for meal delivery from my favorite restaurant.

What I needed in a mental health 911 moment as a suicidal teenager looked a lot different from what supports me today during a season of heightened anxiety. Not only am I further into my healing journey with dramatically improved circumstances, but I've also had time to hone my coping skills.

2. Build a tiered support network.

Before building a network of individuals I knew I could rely on, I was leaning on the same one to two people time and time again. It didn't take long for me to recognize the demand I was placing on their time and emotions. Without meaning to, I was requiring more of my friends and family than they had to offer.

Like us, our loved ones have their own families, struggles, jobs, and "stuff" they are dealing with. And like us, they have their limits on how much they can pour into someone before they need to recharge. No matter how much our friends and family may want to love and support us, they only have so much physical and mental energy in their bucket before it runs dry. So, with this realization in mind, I saw the need to expand my support base—while honing my own self-help skills—which in turn gave me a greater sense of confidence and independence. I saw that with the right support and coping skills, there were some situations I could navigate individually with my therapist and other situations I could actually handle on my own.

When you begin to build your support network, each member will serve a different purpose and strengthen you in their own unique way. In my opinion, the more people, places, and things that can help you when you're in a tough spot, the better! Each of my "Team Tabitha" members has a unique way of helping and supporting me. Some of them offer to watch my kids when I'm overloaded at work, knowing I homeschool them and rarely get quiet time to focus. Others are my prayer warriors. I know that at any time—day or night—I can reach out and they will immediately intercede for me. Some are my cheering section. Whenever something goes well for me, I can count on them to be some of the first to notice. A few are my shoulder to cry on. I cannot tell you how many times, even through the writing of this book, I would leave sobbing Facebook voice messages for my friends to listen to at their leisure, and even if it was days later, they'd circle back around to speak encouraging truths into my circumstances.

Instead of relying solely on just one person and potentially putting a strain on our relationship, I benefit from the strength and giftings of an entire community. Likewise, I strive to be a great team member to my friends as well. Every support network looks a little different, but here is a hypothetical list to get you started:

- God
- Counselor
- Partner or parents
- 2-4 trusted friends
- Pastor or mentor
- Ministry partners (friends in similar ministries or positions who understand the weight you carry)

3. Develop effective self-soothing techniques.

The more I've healed, the more I've learned that support isn't always found *only* in a person. Sometimes, help is found in places, sounds, sights, and smells that calm me down and center me. When I find myself being mentally pulled in a direction I don't want to go, I can always hop in my truck, roll the windows down, blast country music, and go for a long drive to settle my soul. Or I can light a lavender-scented candle, put some worship music on Pandora, and close myself off from the world long enough to think and pray through whatever is upsetting me. Others may find activities like exercise classes or running to be therapeutic. (No running for me; if you see me running, you should probably run, too, because something's chasing me!)

This is especially important because unfortunately, we don't always have access to healthy relationships. I certainly didn't at many times in my life, which is why I relied so heavily on God, my therapist, and self-soothing techniques such as:

- Comforting or self-help books and/or podcasts that encourage and strengthen you
- Prayer
- Calming places or activities
- Long drives or walks
- Grounding techniques such as taking ten slow deep breaths, focusing on your senses, or stretching
- Mindfulness practices such as gratitude, meditation, body scans, and sensory exercises
- Journaling
- Working out
- Spending time in nature

While I know it's hard to trust people, one of the most significant parts of my healing was accepting the risk that comes with being vulnerable. Through that vulnerability, I have found that there are so many people in this world who want to help you along in your healing journey as they listen to, pray for, and cheer for you.

4. Stay grounded in God's truth.

Earlier in this chapter I asked you to make a list of who you think you are: your character traits, strengths, skills, hobbies, likes, and interests. Now that you've made your list about who *you* say you are, it's time to build on that positive list with who *God* says you are. The next time the enemy tries to tell you, "You're worthless. You're a burden. They're better off without you," speak out these truths about who you are in Christ:

I am redeemed.
In Him we have redemption through His blood,
the forgiveness of sins, according to the riches of
His grace.
(Ephesians 1:7 NKJV)

I am worth dying for.
God showed his great love for us by sending Christ
to die for us while we were still sinners.
(Romans 5:8 NLT)

I am called.
Let each person lead the life that the Lord
has assigned to him, and to which God has
called him.
(1 Corinthians 7:17)

I am safe.
In peace [and with a tranquil heart] I will both lie
down and sleep,
For You alone, O LORD, make me dwell in
safety *and* confident trust.
(Psalm 4:8 AMP)

I am protected.
The Lord is faithful, and he will strengthen you and
protect you from the evil one.
    (2 Thessalonians 3:3 NIV)

I am loved.
See what great love the Father has lavished on us,
that we should be called children of God! And that is
what we are!
    (1 John 3:1 NIV)

I am victorious.
In all these things we are more than conquerors
through him who loved us.
    (Romans 8:37)

I have a good future ahead of me.
"For I know the plans I have for you," declares the
LORD, "plans to prosper you and not to harm you,
plans to give you hope and a future."
    (Jeremiah 29:11 NIV)

I am accepted.
Accept each other just as Christ has accepted you so
that God will be given glory.
    (Romans 15:7 NLT)

I am precious.
Since you were precious in My sight,
You have been honored,
and I have loved you.
    (Isaiah 43:4 NKJV)

I am God's.

The Lord who created you, O Israel, says: Don't be afraid, for I have ransomed you; I have called you by name; you are mine.

(Isaiah 43:1 TLB)

Place this list somewhere where you will see it *every* day. Satan, the father of lies (John 8:44), works overtime to convince us that the falsehoods we've believed about ourselves are true. We must tune in to God's gentle whispers about who we are in Him to silence the lies coming at us from every side.

The next time intrusive thoughts start creeping in—of you being a burden, no one caring about what happens to you, or people being better off without you—take a deep breath and evaluate what led to those feelings. Is there something you can change to help you not feel so heavy? Perhaps a relationship needs to go, a self-belief needs to be altered, or a support network needs to be broadened. If you see areas where things need to be adjusted, know that you don't have to change everything at once. Simply take small steps forward to implement that change. However, if upon reflection you find that the root of your feelings is out of your control, release yourself from the weight of blame. Stop beating yourself up for symptoms that aren't your fault or a diagnosis that wasn't your choice. Treat yourself with the same kindness and grace you'd show a beloved friend.

Now that you've done the necessary self-evaluation, it's time to remind yourself of the good you have to offer the world. You are here for a reason, and no one can take that away. God's purpose for you is greater than you could even imagine, and I can't wait to hear about all the wonderful ways He's going to use your story to help others heal.

By having these four essential items to support your mental health—a mental health first aid kit, a varied support network, effective self-soothing techniques, and a list of God's truths—you'll be equipping yourself with as many tools as possible that you can pull out and use when you find your mind going to a dark place or when you're being led to believe you are a burden to others.

I used to scoff when people would tell me that "it gets better." But now I absolutely know that to be true. I also know that it doesn't randomly occur. It gets better when we focus on our emotional well-being. It gets better when we find the proper support, both in faith and mental health communities. It gets better when we stop running from our trauma and instead sit with it. It gets better when we learn more coping strategies in therapy and apply them to our lives. And it gets better when we train our minds to dwell on the truth that Jesus promises in His word.

Jesus and Therapy

Jesus

Write down one sentence of truth that God's Word says about you that you have a difficult time believing. Maybe it's hard for you to believe that you are loved by the Creator. Maybe you struggle to trust that God has good plans for your future. Perhaps you believe that redemption exists for everyone but you. Take a few moments to soak in all the things that God has to say about your identity in Him (you can refer to the statements and verses listed on pages 132–134 and pray that you will be able to walk in the confidence that comes from knowing—and believing—you truly belong.

Therapy

In your next therapy session, explore questions like, *How do I currently feel about myself? How do I want to feel about myself? In what ways have my past experiences made me more inclined to believe I'm a burden to those around me?* The way you talk to yourself matters. Work with your therapist to implement tools that will help you speak value and purpose over your life.

Ten

God Uses Broken People to Reach Broken People

Examining Mental Health in the Bible

> God is looking for broken men, for men who have judged themselves in the light of the Cross of Christ. When He wants anything done, He takes up men who have come to an end of themselves, and whose trust and confidence is not in themselves but in God.
>
> —HARRY A. IRONSIDE, "BROKEN VESSELS FOR CHRIST"

From my earliest memories, and extending well into my thirties, three falsehoods kept me trapped in shame, isolated from other Christians, angry at God, and hiding the light He always intended for me to shine. Perhaps they'll sound familiar to you.

1. You will only have a testimony if you made it through the test.

How will I ever be able to help anyone if I struggle with anxiety for the rest of my life? I wondered. *What kind of encouragement would that testimony be?* Convinced that

I would never be of any use to those around me, I kept my head down and my mouth shut rather than boldly declaring the work God was doing *through* my hardships and trials. The truth is that we all have issues, whether in our past or our present, and not for one second does that limit the good that God can do in us and through us.

2. You're the only one this messed up.

Throughout my life, I've bought into some of the most persistent lies that anxiety and depression can tell you. You know, the ones that make you feel as if you're alone on a deserted island: *No one else understands. I'm the only one who feels this way. No one would respect me if they knew my darkest moments.* But guess what? We're all broken, my friend. The enemy has kept too many of us isolated and hiding from fulfilling our God-given purpose by keeping us bound by shame. Let's not be another statistic. When we walk in freedom and redemption, confident of who God has called us to be, we are a true threat to the powers of darkness in this world.

3. God has caused all my suffering.

At some point, we're all going to have to walk through a valley we don't want to. That valley might include abuse, family dysfunction, disease, addiction, or broken relationships. Growing up, I didn't see valleys as a normal part of life. Instead, Christians ingrained in me that all my sufferings were caused by God in an effort to either punish me or teach me a lesson. Care to venture a guess as to how angry I was at God after all the years of pain I had endured? My rage was nearly insurmountable.

Even if we overcome lies 1 and 2, the longer we're stuck in our anger and bitterness over the course our life has taken, the less we are willing to allow God to work through our weaknesses and struggles. Because these three beliefs were the hardest for me to break free from, we're going to spend the rest of the chapter dismantling them.

If you're still feeling alone in your struggles, or you find it hard to believe that God wants to use you regardless of what darkness you are walking through, or you're having trouble understanding that He isn't the source of your pain, the rest of this chapter is for you. We're going to dive into the Bible as we read about a few of the unlikely people God used to accomplish His purposes on earth. Bible times were many centuries ago and mental health was likely not a phrase ever uttered or understood. Yet we can look back at many examples where people suffered from anxiety, depression, burnout, self-harm, grief, and despair, just as we do now.

The stories below were chosen with great intention to illustrate the range of weaknesses and struggles experienced by other believers, as well as the variety of causes from which their suffering stemmed. We'll witness individuals in the Bible who suffered from challenging circumstances in their life (Job); wrong done to them that was no fault of their own (Joseph); natural consequences of sin (David); as well as those who suffered because they turned their back on Jesus (Peter). Like these biblical heroes of the faith, people today experience hardship, pain, sickness, mental distress, and even death. Suffering is not always by choice or associated with fault; neither is it a result of God desiring His children to suffer.

My prayer is that by the time you reach the end of this list, you'll see yourself among these broken people whom God has used for generations to reach other hurting people. If He had a place at His table for me and all these individuals we're about to discuss, I don't doubt for a moment that there's a seat with your name on it. God is not recruiting from the pedestals. He is reaching into the pits, lifting you up and calling you out to be a living testimony of His goodness, faithfulness, and glory.

Job

Depression comes in many forms. There's depression rooted in trauma and depression stemming from a chemical imbalance. And then there's circumstantial depression, when the losses, grief, and hardships just keep piling up, and as a result, you feel a deep and ever-present sadness. Enter our friend Job. Boy, oh boy, if anyone ever had a reason to hate life, it would have been Job, right? This devoted follower of Jesus endured more loss in a single day than any of us have ever known through our entire lifetimes. The Bible recounts this in Job 1:13-21:

> Now there was a day when his sons and daughters were eating and drinking wine in their oldest brother's house, and there came a messenger to Job and said, "The oxen were plowing and the donkeys feeding beside them, and the Sabeans fell upon them and took them and struck down the servants with the edge of the sword, and I alone have escaped to tell you." While he was yet speaking, there came another and said, "The fire of God fell from heaven and burned up the sheep and the servants and consumed them, and I alone have escaped to tell you." While he was yet speaking, there came another and said, "The Chaldeans formed three groups and made a raid

on the camels and took them and struck down the servants with the edge of the sword, and I alone have escaped to tell you." While he was yet speaking, there came another and said, "Your sons and daughters were eating and drinking wine in their oldest brother's house, and behold, a great wind came across the wilderness and struck the four corners of the house, and it fell upon the young people, and they are dead, and I alone have escaped to tell you."

Then Job arose and tore his robe and shaved his head and fell on the ground and worshiped. And he said, "Naked I came from my mother's womb, and naked shall I return. The LORD gave, and the LORD has taken away; blessed be the name of the LORD."

So, to recap, Job lost his livelihood, animals, servants, and *all* his children on the *same* day. I think it's safe to say that if any of us had to face loss of such magnitude, we'd be asking, *Why me, God?* But in all his grief, Job refused to curse God.

Angry that his plan to turn Job away from God didn't work, Satan asked God for permission to take away Job's health, taunting Him that Job had only remained faithful because he still had his health. God agreed, and in the next scene, we see Job afflicted with painful sores from the top of his head to the soles of his feet.

Now, just when we're thinking, *Wow! I could never have Job's kind of faith. How did he not get angry at God? Why didn't he question Him? Curse Him? Run away?* Job's composure started to crack. By the third chapter of the book, he finally spoke out about his despair. Cursing the day of his birth, Job cried out, wishing he could take back his very existence to avoid his current dilemma: "Why did I not die at birth, come out from the womb and expire?" (3:11). Sounds familiar, doesn't it?

Then, as Job sat in the ashes of who he once was, his friends came along, only to cast blame. As we looked at in chapter 3, they implied that Job must have done something to cause the horrors that had befallen him and his family. Even his wife told him to curse God and die (2:9). Can you imagine what an alienating and painful time this was for Job?

Job's cries for justice and for God to hear him continue throughout the remainder of the book of Job. Yet despite the depths of darkness, loss was not the end of Job's story. God restored all that was lost and gave Job twice what he had before. Job 42:12 says, "And the LORD blessed the latter days of Job more than Job's beginning." Job 42:17 states that Job died an old man "full of days."

As it is for us, Job's story wasn't over; redemption and restoration were always part of God's plan. Job's experiences teach us some valuable takeaways:

- Sometimes the hard things we go through are not punishments. It's important to remember that we face opposition from the enemy when we're seeking to honor God with our lives.
- God doesn't condemn our times of brokenness before Him.
- God's not threatened by our anger, and He doesn't hide His face from us, even when we're cursing the skies.
- There is a redemptive solution to every trial, loss, and pain we face.

Martha

Martha was what we would call in modern times a "worrywart." She had an anxious mind—always going, always doing, always worried about something or other.

What I love about Martha's story is that Jesus didn't shun her or get upset about her concerns. The Bible makes it clear that Martha was a friend of Jesus—so much so that we see multiple accounts in scripture of her talking to Him in a way many of us could not imagine doing.

In the book of Luke, we read about Martha hosting guests in her home. Busy with preparations, it's obvious she was flustered and upset that her sister, Mary, was not helping her serve. Imagine her coming up to her friend Jesus in a bit of a huff and saying: "Lord, do you not care that my sister has left me to serve alone? Tell her then to help me" (Luke 10:40).

First, Martha was like, "Do you even care, Jesus?" Then she straight up told Him what to do! If I were her, I'd be looking around for an impending lightning strike. But instead of responding in anger to Martha's insinuation and demand, Jesus gently chided her, saying: "Martha, Martha! You are worried and upset about so many things, but only one thing is necessary. Mary has chosen what is best, and it will not be taken away from her" (Luke 10:41-42 CEV).

I love that Jesus acknowledged Martha's emotions and then lovingly prodded her back toward the most important thing—a relationship with Him.

This is not the only time Martha was brutally honest with Jesus. Following the death of her brother, Lazarus, in John 11, we see the sisters send a message to Jesus telling him their brother was ill. While Jesus seemed to take His own sweet time getting there, Lazarus passed. Holding nothing back, we once again see Martha tell Jesus exactly how she feels: "Lord, if you had been here, my brother would not have died. But even now I know that whatever you ask from God, God will give you" (John 11:21-22).

Is it just me, or do Martha's words sound like she was blaming Jesus? *If You'd been here, this wouldn't have happened.* But Jesus knew Martha's heart. He knew that her faith in Him outweighed all the unfiltered, anxious questions coming out of her mouth. Jesus's response to Martha lashing out in her grief was both simple and profound. We see in the book of John, in the shortest verse in the Bible, "Jesus wept" (John 11:35). What a beautiful glimpse into our Savior's kindness as He patiently responded to Martha's questions—and even her anger.

Despite knowing that He was about to bring Lazarus back to life, Jesus still acknowledged Martha's pain. It still mattered to Him. It would have been easy for Him to discount Martha's despair, to tell her that if she had faith in Him, she wouldn't be worried or saddened. After all, if she truly believed Jesus had the power to raise her brother from the dead, what was she even crying for? But that's not the example Jesus gave us here. We see Him weep with the hurting, despite their doubt and fear. Because of Jesus's response, we can take away several important truths from Martha's story:

- Martha was close to Jesus and knew Him in a deeply personal way, yet she still suffered from anxiety.
- In the midst of Martha's worry and grief, she maintained a strong faith.
- Jesus never condemned Martha's authenticity in her conversations with Him.
- Jesus grieved with Martha and was empathetic to her feelings.

Paul

Paul was one of the most influential disciples in the New Testament, writing thirteen books of the Bible. He willingly suffered for Jesus. He was imprisoned for his faith, and historians believe the Romans beheaded him for his unapologetic following of Jesus. But before Paul was all these things, he was Saul—a Pharisee, a hypocrite, and a godless man who tracked down Christians to torment them and put them to death. In 1 Timothy 1:15, Paul went as far as to call his former self the "chief" of sinners (NKJV). If you ever needed a figure in the Bible to make you believe in the power of redemption, you'll find it in Paul.

One of the great things about Paul's writings is his honesty about his struggles with sin, infirmities, hunger, weakness, and so much more. As we read in Romans 7:15, he wrestled constantly against his own human nature and propensity to sin: "I do not understand my own actions. For I do not do what I want, but I do the very thing I hate."

In 2 Corinthians 12:7-10, we learn that Paul also suffered from a physical ailment that God refused to remove from him:

> . . . A thorn was given me in the flesh, a messenger of Satan to harass me, to keep me from becoming conceited. Three times I pleaded with the Lord about this, that it should leave me. But he said to me, "My grace is sufficient for you, for my power is made perfect in weakness." Therefore, I will boast all the more gladly of my weaknesses, so that the power of Christ may rest upon me. For the sake of Christ, then, I am content with weaknesses, insults, hardships, persecutions, and calamities. For when I am weak, then I am strong.

145

Throughout the New Testament, we read about Paul surviving one terrible trial after another, whether a stoning, a beating, jail time, or even a shipwreck. Yet despite this guy's life being no walk in the park, he never stopped chasing after Jesus. Paul had seen life without Jesus and never wanted to return to that reality again.

It speaks to the depths of Paul's faith to know that in the face of such great suffering, he chose to follow Jesus over the world. In 2 Corinthians 1:8, even the great disciple Paul reached such a point of despair that he wanted to give up on life: "We do not want you to be unaware, brothers and sisters, of the affliction we experienced. . . . For we were so utterly burdened beyond our strength that we despaired of life itself." This giant in the faith, used greatly by the Lord, became so weary of the troubles in this broken world that he wanted to throw in the towel.

Though Paul was pressed physically and mentally beyond what he felt he could endure, God still used him in a mighty way. Paul's life teaches us many things:

- No follower of Christ is immune from a life of chronic struggle or pain.
- Authenticity in communication plays an important role in ministry.
- God does sometimes give us more than we can physically or mentally handle, because we weren't meant to handle it without Him and the body of Christ.
- Jesus is the safest place to take our pain.

Elijah

Elijah was a man of God, a prophet whom God used to speak on His behalf. Because of Elijah's prayers, God held back rain for three and a half years. For crying out loud, God used Elijah to raise the dead and to call down fire from Heaven! Still, even as God's chosen instrument who performed miracle after miracle, Elijah struggled with a deep depression.

After Queen Jezebel vowed to kill Elijah, we see this formerly bold prophet of God running for his life, absolutely terrified. Not hard to imagine, right? Then, tired of trying so hard just to survive, Elijah collapses under a tree. He'd lost what little fight he had left. We are told in 1 Kings 19:4, "Then he went on alone into the wilderness, traveling all day. He sat down under a solitary broom tree and prayed that he might die. 'I have had enough, LORD,' he said. 'Take my life'" (NLT).

Now, if you or I had just watched God perform all kinds of miracles through us, then we plopped down and declared that we wanted to die, can you imagine the responses we might get? I guarantee you that some of the "Christian" responses would be: "What a disgrace that after all the ways you've seen God move, your faith is so weak," or, "You used to be such a strong Christian. It's so sad to see you backslide." But God knew Elijah was human, and instead of responding to His servant's depression in judgment, anger, or impatience, God sent an angel to feed and comfort him. Here's what we can glean from Elijah's story:

- We can love Jesus, be used by Him in radical ways, and still be suicidal.
- Mental health challenges are not synonymous with weak faith.
- Exhaustion and burnout can lead us to dark places mentally. Sometimes, we simply need rest.

- Jesus has a whole health approach to our needs. He didn't send an angel to preach to Elijah. He sent one to feed and comfort him. Part of healing means addressing our physical needs and deficits.

David

David was many things in the Bible—a shepherd, a giant slayer, a poet, a musician, and a king. He was also an adulterer, a liar, and a murderer. David strove to chase after the Lord, but he often got sidetracked chasing things God didn't want for him, and he paid a price for his choices. Still, despite his sins, David had a repentant heart. He was so pained by how he'd grieved the heart of God that he cried out for mercy in the Psalms: "Have mercy on me, O God, according to your steadfast love; according to your abundant mercy blot out my transgressions. Wash me thoroughly from my iniquity and cleanse me from my sin!" (Psalm 51:1-2).

David represents the prodigal in many of us. Sometimes in our wanderings, we make choices that have consequences that hurt us and those around us. There certainly is such a thing as circumstantial depression and despair, and in David's case, some of his inner turmoil directly correlated to his own poor decisions. Yet even then God did not forsake or abandon David to wallow in the pit he'd quite clearly dug for himself.

Despite how far David strayed from God's path, God's grace was always there for him to throw himself upon. In Acts 13:22 the Lord declared, "I have found David son of Jesse, a man after my own heart. He will do everything I want him to do" (NLT). From a man with blood on his hands to a man after God's own heart—only God can transform us like that!

Through David's life, we learn:

- It's never too late to shift course. God always forgives us and eagerly welcomes us back.

- Even if our own sins or mistakes brought on our suffering, God freely gives us access to His grace.

- Brutal honesty and broken hallelujahs are often the deepest forms of worship. God would rather have us turn *to* Him in our mess and our pain than be driven away from Him.

- Our pasts do not define or dictate our current standing with Jesus or limit how He can use us.

Peter

A fisherman by trade, Peter experienced Jesus up close and personal. When Jesus called him to be one of His disciples, He told Peter that He would make him a fisher ... of men. Out of all the disciples, Peter is the one who had the faith and trust in Jesus to step out of the boat and walk on water. It was Peter who first declared publicly that Jesus was the Messiah. By all accounts, Peter would have done anything for Jesus, including sacrificing his own life.

Given Peter's history, it's baffling then that he would go on to deny Jesus at the crucifixion. After all they had been through together and all the miracles, Peter denied Christ not just once but *three times*. I mean, Peter *knew* that he *knew* that Jesus was the Son of God, yet he turned his back on Him in Jesus's darkest moment. Seems pretty unforgivable, right? Not for Jesus.

Following His resurrection, Jesus appeared to some of the disciples, including Peter. Now, if it were me, I would be planning to give Peter a piece of my mind! But instead of being angry or berating Peter for denying Him, Jesus fed him breakfast. He just wanted Peter's heart. As if to allude to Peter's three denials, In John 21:15-19, we see Jesus question Peter three times about his love for Him:

> When they had finished breakfast, Jesus said to Simon Peter, "Simon, son of John, do you love me more than these?" He said to him, "Yes, Lord; you know that I love you." He said to him, "Feed my lambs." He said to him a second time, "Simon, son of John, do you love me?" He said to him, "Yes, Lord; you know that I love you." He said to him, "Tend my sheep." He said to him the third time, "Simon, son of John, do you love me?" Peter was grieved because he said to him the third time, "Do you love me?" and he said to him, "Lord, you know everything; you know that I love you." Jesus said to him, "Feed my sheep." . . . And after saying this he said to him, "Follow me."

Wait, did I miss something? There was no sharp rebuke, no "I'm so disappointed in you," no punishment, just simply, "Do you love me? OK, follow me." Instead of letting Peter wallow in the despair that surely consumed him following his rejection of the son of God, Jesus invited Peter into a relationship with Him. If you, like me, have flat-out denied God's existence, even cursed it, and your shame has kept you from throwing yourself at the feet of Jesus, you will not find any condemnation waiting. Simply invite Christ into your life and allow Him to take the lead. You can start today.

Peter's life demonstrates:

- Denying God doesn't disqualify us from a future relationship with Him.

- Scripture makes it abundantly clear that God loves to choose and use people whom the world deems unfit or unlikely.
- Jesus is faithful when we are faithless.
- In Christ, there is enough compassion and divine forgiveness to cover the return of any prodigal.

Joseph

Joseph had a golden childhood. Unfortunately for him, the favor his parents showed him eventually caused his older brothers to resent him terribly. One day when Joseph's brothers saw him coming, they plotted to kill him. Hoping to save his little brother's life, Joseph's oldest brother, Reuben, suggested throwing Joseph into a pit instead of outright killing him. Agreeing to Reuben's plan, the other brothers stripped Joseph of his coat and cast him into the pit. When Reuben returned to rescue Joseph, he found the pit empty and Joseph gone. The other brothers had sold Joseph into slavery. This was just the first of many circumstances Joseph found himself in that were completely out of his control.

After being sold as a slave in Egypt, Joseph was given a respectable position as head of household for Potiphar, the captain of Pharaoh's guard. People took notice of young Joseph, including Potiphar's wife, who tried to entice him. Unwilling to betray his master, Joseph refused her. Angry at Joseph's rejection, Potiphar's wife claimed Joseph had tried to rape her. Believing his wife's lies, Potiphar threw Joseph in prison. *Again*, Joseph suffered at the hands of others' wrongdoing. Having *every reason* to be angry at the injustices that continued to befall him, Joseph instead seemed to remain a man of character. His integrity made him stand out in every position he was placed in. Even in prison, he was appointed as the warden's right-hand man.

Joseph eventually got some unexpected company in prison when Pharoah's chief cupbearer and baker were thrown into jail with him. They must have made friends with Joseph because when the two men were haunted by dreams they couldn't explain, they went straight to Joseph for help. Having previously been hated by his brothers for his own dreams, I'm guessing Joseph wasn't in a hurry to interpret anyone else's. With God's help, however, Joseph accurately deciphered both dreams. Three days later, the cupbearer was freed to return to his position working with the king, as Joseph's interpretation predicted. Finally! Would this be Joseph's chance at freedom? Nope! Joseph was forgotten and imprisoned for two more years. The guy couldn't get a break.

Regardless of how badly everything seemed to go for poor Joseph, God had not forgotten him. There was about to be another dream that would change the course of Joseph's story. One day, when all the wise men of Egypt failed to interpret a distressing dream for Pharaoh, the chief cupbearer finally remembered his old pal, Joseph, who'd just celebrated his thirtieth birthday in prison. When Joseph's interpretation of the king's dream saved the entire nation, Pharoah did the unthinkable, as we see in Genesis 41:39-40 (NLT):

> Then Pharoah said to Joseph, "Since God has revealed the meaning of the dreams to you, clearly no one else is as intelligent or wise as you are. You will be in charge of my court, and all my people will take orders from you. Only I, sitting on my throne, will have a rank higher than yours."

Seeing that God's spirit was upon Joseph, Pharaoh blessed Joseph with a position second only to his own, a new name—*Zaphenath-Paneah*—which means "God speaks and lives," and a beautiful wife. As time passed, God brought even more redemption to Joseph, blessing him with children and eventually the opportunity to reconcile with his brothers.

We can see through Joseph's struggles that:

- We have a choice regarding how to respond to unjust situations that happen to us.
- Seasons of hardship can last for many years, even decades, and still result in miraculous restoration.
- Just because God works all things for our ultimate good doesn't mean it will feel good in the middle of the trial.
- Jesus can take what was meant to destroy us and use it to save countless others.

If you've lived a life that makes you nod along with Joseph's story, where at every turn another person hurts you, another injustice occurs, and you feel as though you've been living at rock bottom for far too long, I have good news: God has not forsaken you. In fact, God wasn't far from any of the people we've discussed in this chapter. He never left them, not once, though each of them likely felt abandoned at one point.

God saw a bigger picture than Joseph could see in his humanity. If Joseph hadn't been thrown in the pit, sold into slavery, and then thrown into jail, how could God have used him to save the people of Egypt? Joseph not only had his life restored tenfold, but his trials enabled him to save countless others due to the wisdom and favor God eventually gave him.

In the same way, you and I have learned valuable lessons in our pain. Perhaps you haven't found your ultimate redemptive purpose yet or even caught a glimpse of it. And maybe you're still in your pit or your prison and can't see the light at the end of the tunnel in this season you feel stuck in. Even so, I am convinced that God will turn your wounds into wisdom, and it isn't a question of if, but when. He is still the same God today as He was in the time of Joseph, as well as the time of Martha, Paul, Elijah, David, and Peter. He still holds the power over death and depression. He still offers the same promise of redemption to you and me that no hardship we experience will ever be wasted.

Jesus and Therapy

Jesus

Thank God that He is the same yesterday, today, and forever. As you reflect on the stories above, pray for Him to break the chains of shame that have held you back from sharing your testimony, even as it is still unfolding. Ask the Lord to impress on your heart which of these biblical characters most mirrors your story, what hope you can glean from them, and how you can cling to their experiences.

Therapy

If you've felt isolated in your struggles, see if your counselor knows of any peer support groups or mentorship programs that might be a good fit for your journey. In addition, ask for book or podcast recommendations that feature someone who's made it to the other side of similar situations you're currently going through.

Eleven

Church Hurt

Recovery and Reconstruction

> The church is not a select circle of the immaculate, but a home where the outcast may come in. It is not a palace with gate attendants and challenging sentinels along the entranceways holding off at arm's-length the stranger, but rather a hospital where the broken-hearted may be healed, and where all the weary and troubled may find rest and take counsel together.
>
> —JAMES H. AUGHEY, *SPIRITUAL GEMS OF THE AGES*

There was a time when I fully believed I'd never engage in organized religion again. And for years, I didn't. It took me decades to separate Christ from Christianity. My view of who God was and how He loved me had been tainted by the abuse and mistreatment I suffered at the hands of flawed "believers" who were completely out of touch with God's heart. It took most of my life to land anywhere near a healthy perspective on church and to begin engaging with other Christians in a meaningful way.

I realized that many of the things religion had told me were built on lies I had to systematically dismantle one by one.

- Religion told me to hide from God. Jesus called me out of the shadows and into His glorious light.

- Religion told me I would never be good enough. Jesus told me I didn't have to be good. His finished work on the cross called me to come as I was.

- Religion told me to try harder. Jesus invited me to rest in His truth that my salvation wasn't earned based on merit.

- Religion condemned me. Jesus called me precious and honored in His sight.

- Religion called me unclean. Jesus called me redeemed and sanctified—not because of who I am, but Whose I am.

- Religion sought to punish me. Jesus stepped in front of me and dared he who was without sin to cast the first stone.

- Religion placed me on the outside. Jesus welcomed me in.

Perhaps today you find yourself where I was back then, desperate to discover where religion ends and Jesus begins. Maybe the pain from wounding messages received from people of faith feels as fresh as if it happened yesterday, and the anger over it all feels like it's going to eat you alive. I wish I didn't, but I understand how you feel. For years, everything that had been said and done to me played over and over in my head like a bad movie scene. The anger was so all-consuming that my only release was to go outside to scream at the sky, punch my bedroom walls, or hurl a glass across the concrete just to watch it shatter. I couldn't even seem to sleep without mentally rehearsing all the things I wish I'd said to my abusers. If I could only find my voice, I told myself I'd use it to stand up for all the injustices I'd endured.

The Art of Letting Go

When I reflect on my time in the "trenches," I wish more than anything that I could go back for no other reason but to let go of my anger sooner. Living in that bitterness and despair cost me dearly, from physical illness to constant suicidal ideation. Instead of punishing my abusers, reliving the pain hurt *me*, ensuring I wouldn't heal or move past the trauma. Knowing what I know now, if I could do it over again, I'd use every ounce of that emotional energy to chase after the freedom from trauma I deserved. Instead, my refusal to let go gave power over me to those who couldn't have cared less about the damage they'd inflicted.

Healing from church hurt is not as simple as it sounds. The mending is messy, and it takes time—sometimes more time than we'd like. For healing to occur, we must be willing to let go of our anger, bitterness, rejection, and pain. You are worthy of a life free from the wounds caused by the careless words and actions of broken souls. Instead of staying stuck in that vicious cycle of negative emotions, why not chase healing and the life of purpose God intended for you?

Healing looks different for everyone, and though the wounding in your story is uniquely yours, I believe we can all benefit from walking through the steps below on our road to wholeness.

1. Acknowledge the pain.

In my situation, there was *so* much victim-shaming, gaslighting, and blame-shifting that I was unable to call the abuse what it was or acknowledge the hurt that my church had caused. After all, my childhood had taught me that staying quiet was the only way to keep any measure of peace. As you can imagine, staying silent and ignoring the pain didn't exactly facilitate healing—it kept me sick.

There's a wide spectrum to choose from on the "church hurt" scale. For some of us, that scale includes being blamed for our diagnosis or being told that our circumstances are a punishment from God. For others of us, our "church hurt" is wrapped up in being raised in a church so legalistic that, to this day, we feel like we can hardly breathe without being judged. Your experience could have ranged from hurtful words spoken to you to abuse you experienced at the hands of church members.

Regardless of how you were wounded, there is power in calling the abuse or pain what it was and saying it out loud. Trying to sugarcoat what you went through in an effort to not offend anyone is not conducive to healing. Acknowledge just how painful your interactions with the church or Christianity were to you. That truly is the first step. While this action may sound easy, it can come at a cost. In fact, I learned that if I wanted to heal, I had to be willing to lose some relationships, at least for a time. Not everyone in my life was at the same stage of healing that I was, where they felt the freedom to bring the truth into the light and talk openly about the past.

2. Separate yourself from continual sources of pain.

Imagine you have an open wound that just won't heal because somebody keeps ripping off the bandage, pouring lemon juice on it, and poking it. All you want to do is start the recovery process, but that poor wound is still as bloody as the first day the injury occurred. In this regard, emotional wounds are a lot like physical wounds. Unless we distance ourselves from what's habitually hurting us, we'll focus on the most recent painful interaction and wounding message received rather than directing our time and energy toward healing. Our bodies and minds need time and space to address those foundational wounds because their roots run *deep*. If you're anything like me, those wounds will take time to heal because they're intrinsically woven into your core beliefs about yourself and your faith.

Once we've removed ourselves from our unhealthy environment, we can begin to pursue closure and assess the damage. As difficult as it may be, it's often necessary to block off those toxic individuals' access to us. It's hard work to draw healthy boundaries and, in many cases, protect ourselves from future abuse, while also giving ourselves time to recover.

3. Face everything.

By the time I reached my thirties, I had more anger to work through than I knew what to do with because it had been stifled for so long. Whether you're trying to protect a loved one's emotions or trying not to rock the boat, it's not doing anyone any good to keep those emotions buried. You do not owe a single person your silence.

One of the most healing things we can do is learn to sit with our emotions and stop running from them. It takes time to work up to the simple act of being OK with the silence, especially if we're used to numbing ourselves with alcohol, food, medication, television, and other coping mechanisms. But we can't outrun the pain forever, can we? I spent years upon years running because I couldn't face the magnitude of the suffering built up within me. Eventually, attempting to escape my emotions became an exhausting and futile cycle I was determined to break free from. I learned that the screams I tried to drown out were simply those of a younger self, crying to finally be heard. Placing photos of myself as a child on my wall to look at every single day was the reminder I needed to sit with the crushing pain and memories, so my inner child would no longer have to hold on to them for me. She deserved that from me.

For your sake, I hope you can gradually face the feelings you've been avoiding so you can acknowledge them, validate them, work through them, and release them. The next time an uncomfortable emotion arises within you, give yourself verbal permission to feel it. *I am allowed to feel . . . angry, hurt, betrayed . . . (fill in the blank).* This is one of the kindest things you can do for yourself: remind yourself that you are free to feel all that you may have been forced or pressured to stifle throughout your life.

4. Give yourself grace to walk through the journey of healing.

Healing is not instant, nor is it linear. It's messy and hard, but it's undoubtedly worth it. One of my favorite quotes by Adam Bletsoe says, "Healing might feel like breaking at first."[20] Those words resonate deeply with me because when we start dealing with the demons in our past, it can feel like we're free-falling and don't know where we'll land. Growth can be painful when old habits, mindsets, and relationships are being shifted, transformed, or redefined. But as uncomfortable as growth can be, it's never as painful as staying stuck. Stripping away false beliefs and replacing them with

God's truth will take time. Be patient with yourself as you keep moving forward.

5. Identify who hurt you and how.

[Before you consider walking out this step, it's vital that you feel safe and supported. Since digging up old wounds can be traumatic, you may want to do this with the help of a counselor.]

Identifying who wounded you and how they did so is a crucial step in recovery because we cannot face and heal from what we don't recognize and name. We also can't walk through the next step (separating others' actions from God's character) until we tackle this list first. To get started, find a quiet spot where you can journal with minimal distractions. Next, begin to write out who hurt you, what they did, and what lasting wounding message you received.

Often in trauma, the initial abuse or pain is all you can see, but as you slowly release it, another layer of wounding (the secondary hurt) comes to the surface. In order to truly heal, we must recognize all of it. Over the years of healing, I found that secondary hurt can be almost as painful and lasting as the surface wound it was buried beneath. For instance: "Parent A abused me, but Parent B didn't protect me from the abuse," or, "The pastor mistreated me, but I told my guardians or the church leadership, and they didn't do anything about it." As you write, get detailed, if you can. Note every hurtful word, judgment received, and any other abuse that occurred. Put it all down on paper.

6. Separate people's actions from God's character.
Now that you've journaled the specific instances you can recall in which people's actions wounded you, it's time to ask yourself if each event was caused by God or by His people.

For example, as a teenager, I was told no one likes people with depression, and I should just kill myself. That was **the event**. Now, who was **the perpetrator** in that scenario? My father.

After you've made your list and clarified the events and the perpetrators, it's time to examine the wounding message received from each traumatic event and weigh whether they align with the truth of God's Word and His character. The following is one of my personal examples that demonstrates what walking through this process will look like for each item on your list.

The Event: Being told that I wasn't worth saving and even if God could reach me, He wouldn't want to.

The Perpetrator: Elder in my church

The Wounding Message Received: I have exceeded the limits of God's grace. He doesn't love me or want me. He is choosing not to save me because I'm not worth it.

The Truth: • **God's grace is for me.**
(John 1:16, 2 Timothy 1:9, Ephesians 1:7, Romans 5:2, 2 Corinthians 9:8, Hebrews 4:16)

• **God's love for me is boundless.**
(Romans 8:35-39, Ephesians 3:18-19, Psalm 36:5-7, 1 John 3:1, John 3:16)

- **God chose me.**
  (Ephesians 1:5, John 15:16, Jeremiah 1:5, 1 Peter 2:9, 1 Thessalonians 1:4)

- **God's salvation is for me.**
  (Luke 15:4-7, 1 Timothy 2:4, Titus 2:11, Romans 5:8, Romans 10:13)

When our thought process about ourselves and God has been born out of pain rather than truth, resetting how we think is critical. That "reprogramming," if you will, will take a renewing of our minds in God's Word. To put it simply, renewing your mind means interpreting life through the filter of God's truth found in the Bible, rather than through the lens of your own experiences, wounds, and trauma. And unlike what I was taught growing up, God's Word is not intended to bring condemnation, but rather freedom and the truth about who we are in Him.

I urge you to take time to start working on your list as described above to begin rooting out the false wounding messages you've received. Like me, you'll likely find that God's true character doesn't align with how people treated you, nor was it Him they were following when they hurt you. This clarity is crucial to reframing how we view God and to finding the good that is waiting in Him for you.

7. Release the pain.

Many of you have likely heard this saying by Joyce Meyer, but it bears repeating: "Harboring unforgiveness is like drinking poison and hoping your enemy will die."[21] When I look back on my years of walking away from God and Christianity and how angry I was, I was doing just that: drinking poison every darn day and hoping my enemy would die. Instead, the only person slowly dying inside was me. I was stuck holding on to and reliving the pain while my abusers moved forward with their lives, unaffected.

In a best-case scenario, the people who wounded us are repentant and have changed their behavior. On the other hand, they could refuse to acknowledge their wrongdoing, become defensive, shame and gaslight us, and remain completely unapologetic. But here's the good news: after carrying more than my fair share of unforgiveness, I've learned that regardless of what *someone else's* response to a situation is, that response doesn't have to dictate my ability to heal. Whether or not it does is *my* choice.

Too often, we hold on to a painful event because it was a defining moment in our lives. We might believe that by releasing that event, we're letting the person who hurt us "off the hook." I get it. We want them to be sorry. We want them to admit what they did. But what if they never apologize? What if they never acknowledge the pain they caused? We still need to let it go. Why? Because it isn't about them anymore, it's about us. It's about the full, joy-filled life God wants us to take hold of.

You deserve to be released from painful triggers.

You deserve to walk away free.

Holding on is only holding you captive.

Jesus is a just God. He sees all. You can trust Him to deal with your abusers in *His* time. Whether they know it or not, a day will come when they must answer to their Maker for what they did.

Letting go is far easier said than done. It took me a good twenty years in therapy to release the people who forever changed the course of my life. But, as I've already confessed,

I spent much of that time running and numbing. Had I not been so afraid of simply sitting with my feelings and listening to what my pain was trying to tell me, my healing journey might have been a lot less lengthy and messy.

8. Anchor yourself in the truth of who Jesus is.

Throughout this book, we have talked about who you are in Christ, what His character is, and the lengths He'll go to in order to reach you. A few steps ago, we also established who Jesus is not. He's *not* the one who wounded you. He's *not* the God others falsely portrayed Him to be. And He does *not* take delight in your sufferings.

I spent a lot of time believing that I truly knew Jesus. And because I lived a life of legalism and followed every rule known to man, I thought I was pleasing Him. I knew His Word, but not His heart. The truth I finally came to is that I didn't really know God, but I wanted to figure out who He was, how He loved me, and what my purpose was.

The only way you can know God is to spend time with Him. Since starting my healing journey, I have spent countless hours at His feet in worship, in prayer, and in His Word. After you've taken the time to strip away your false beliefs, you will now be looking at a new foundation—an empty space in which to rebuild, a blank page on which to write new truths on your heart. And before we come to any conclusions about who we are, we must first know who He is, because "in him we live and move and have our being" (Acts 17:28).

Here's a brief list to get you started on who Jesus is:

He is good.
(John 10:11, James 1:17)

He is full of mercy.
(Ephesians 2:4, Psalms 145:8)

He extends His grace to all.
(Ephesians 4:7, 2 Timothy 1:9)

He loves me unconditionally.
(Romans 5:6-8, Jeremiah 31:3)

Jesus steps in front of me when the world wants to throw a stone.
(John 8:1-11)

He leaves the ninety-nine just to find me and me alone.
(Matthew 18:12)

He sacrificed everything to be in a relationship with me.
(Romans 8:32, Mark 10:45)

9. Examine your role in the church.

After experiencing being devalued by the body of Christ, you might find it difficult to imagine having a place in the church and a specific role that God has planned for you to fulfill. But are you able to imagine a church with loving, empathetic individuals who are familiar with pain? Can you imagine pews packed with believers who are ready to step in and help others in their struggles or love them exactly where they are?

I was once sitting with someone who had a terminal diagnosis. There was a moment where she simply looked at me and said, "You know pain. That's why I can talk to you." When someone who's facing a tough situation knows you've been about as low as a person can go, there's an automatic level of trust. They've seen you at rock bottom, so they know you won't judge, lecture, or throw a Bible verse at their pain. They know you'll sit and cry with them till the morning comes.

He who is forgiven much loves much, and we prodigals know how to love people, don't we? The body of Christ needs us. We represent the love and acceptance that too many are finding in communities throughout the world but not within the walls of a church home. We know how to look past the mess, the mistakes, and the struggles and see a child deeply loved by God.

There will always be individuals who haven't walked our path or encountered the depth of challenges that led us to the brink of hopelessness, and that's OK. I love them and appreciate their perspectives on life and their faithful walks with the Lord. But just as the church needs what they bring to the table, the church needs what you and I bring as well.

Now that you've seen that God has a role for you in His body, I want you to consider the possibility that after everything you've been through, God may be asking you to step back into a church family. He may be calling you to be the person you needed when you were a kid, whether that's a loving mentor or a godly role model. Ask the Lord to give you wisdom on how you can tangibly show His love to those around you. How can you be a safe place for people to fall? How can you model to others in the body the grace you've been shown?

10. Be intentional about reentering fellowship.
I was a different person by the time I chose to go back to church. I knew who I was. I knew who Jesus was. I knew how I should be treated and what I'd never allow again.

I had healthy boundaries in place, so I didn't fear my interactions with other Christians or church leadership. I knew I was safe. I knew I was stronger.

If the pastor or a fellow Christian stumbled and sinned, my faith wouldn't be shaken because my faith and trust was no longer *in them*. The days of putting another believer on a pedestal were *done*. This foundation of truth enabled me to enter into fellowship again with intentionality, a renewed sense of self, and a love that gave other Christians room to grow.

Many years after returning to church "full time," I realized the reason God commanded us to not forsake the gathering together of believers: we weren't meant to do this life alone. At the risk of sounding cliché, we're stronger together. Gathering with other believers allows our souls to be fed with God's Word, our spirits to be renewed in worship, and our hearts to be encouraged by fellowship. Few things in life are as messy, beautiful, or life-changing as serving and growing alongside fellow believers—as we all chase Jesus together.

For All Have Sinned and Fallen Short

An important thing to note is that a *healthy church* is not a *flawless church*. It is made up entirely of sinful human beings, so there *will* be misunderstandings and people who will sin against us or fail us miserably. *But*, in a healthy body of believers who are in tune with the Holy Spirit, that wounding will not be intentional, and apologies and repentance will be quick when unhealthy behavior is confronted. *A healthy Christian is always willing to receive correction and grow.*

Life isn't neat and tidy, and it doesn't offer us the luxury of a pain-free existence, but it does provide constant opportunities for improvement. Being part of the body of believers means we love each other through that growth.

You'll never meet a person who's not in process—whether that's the pastor of a megachurch, the pope or the president. We all are in process. If I'm following Jesus and pursuing growth, that means the Tabitha you met a year ago hopefully won't look the same as the Tabitha you meet today.

You and I are responsible for ensuring that the Jesus we're portraying to the world looks like the Jesus in the Bible. If a wise friend lovingly points out that our heart or character is not aligned with God's, we need to take a step back, examine our heart, and make a course correction if needed. Otherwise, we not only risk making decisions we'll regret, but we also risk treating others in a way that will turn them away from God rather than draw them to Him.

Church hurt is real, and it occurs every day, but when we learn to put our faith in God and not in flawed humanity, we can better navigate life and relationships within the body of Christ. Believe it or not, that kind of healing is possible without allowing the behaviors, habits, or even the mindsets of the past to dictate our present.

Your voice, compassion, and unique perspective about mental health and Christianity are needed within the body. My prayer for you is that not a soul on this earth would keep you from the place God has set for you at His table with His children. Use the rejection you've faced to fuel your compassion. Let that compassion drive you to be the change you want to see in the church so that everyone feels welcomed by Jesus, no matter their past or their present.

Relationship > Religion

Christ will always choose a relationship with you over a religious institution. In other words, His love is for the believer, not the building. You and I are the church, and He will break through any walls necessary to get to you. Don't allow sinners who hurt you keep you from the Savior who longs to heal you.

I find it incredibly significant that the very last miracle Jesus did before going to the cross was to heal a man whom *His* overzealous disciple injured. Jesus was about to be arrested, and the Bible says, "When the other disciples saw what was about to happen, they exclaimed, 'Lord, should we fight? We brought the swords!' And one of them struck at the high priest's slave, slashing off his right ear. But Jesus said, 'No more of this.' And he touched the man's ear and healed him" (Luke 22:49-51 NLT). In that miracle, Jesus demonstrated that God's heart to heal extends to those who have been struck down and wounded by His own followers. Not only does He reach out to heal the hurt done in His name, but He also tells His sword-wielding disciples, "No more of this."

Jesus and Therapy

Jesus

Wholeness in Christ is a lifelong pursuit. God wants so much more for your life than for you to be stuck ruminating on the pains of your past. Will you prayerfully consider taking the necessary first step of walking through the ways you've been wounded so you don't have to stay captive to or haunted by your past hurts?

Therapy

In this chapter, we've covered ten steps you can take toward healing from church hurt, and every single one of them takes time. With your therapist, discuss which areas of recovery you feel are most relevant to your story. Start with simply one or two that you feel ready to dive into, and allow your counselor to go on this journey with you as you recover from and reevaluate your relationship with the church.

Twelve

Jesus

A Home for the Prodigals

If God didn't hesitate to put everything on the line for us, embracing our condition and exposing himself to the worst by sending his own Son, is there anything else he wouldn't gladly and freely do for us? . . . The One who died for us—who was raised to life for us!—is in the presence of God at this very moment sticking up for us. Do you think anyone is going to be able to drive a wedge between us and Christ's love for us? There is no way!

—Romans 8:31-35 (MSG)

We have spent most of this book discussing the necessity of mental health treatment and how mental health conditions are common within faith-based settings. Both are necessary and important messages to spread. You and I both know that stigmas still exist and the woundings received from those casting judgment on us can last a lifetime. The challenging circumstances and heartbreaking traumas we face in life can cause us emotional pain or mental health challenges through no fault of our own and having nothing to do with a lack of faith.

However, in this chapter, I'm compelled to drive home the "Jesus" component of "Jesus and therapy," because therapy alone will never be enough to heal our deepest wounds. As much as I believe in and advocate for counseling, there comes a point when, despite all the mental health care in the world, we're left with a deep ache. The sadness that never lifts may be because we're warring against our Creator. If we live running away from the only One who gives us true joy, peace, and purpose, then that peace, fulfillment, and true healing will be impossible to find.

I can tell you with absolute certainty that if you've resigned yourself to finding peace outside of faith in Jesus, you won't discover it. It's not there. I should know. After I promised God that I wouldn't under any circumstances become a Christian again, I tried to find something—anything—to fill the bullet holes that "Christianity" had left in me. But during those years that I ran away from God, going as far in the other direction as I could, not a single thing came close to giving me peace. Nothing satisfied my soul or filled the void I couldn't deny was present.

So, my fellow prodigals, perhaps you, like me, have tried to settle for a counterfeit peace. Perhaps you're even placating yourself with the temporal solace this world has to offer. And here's the tricky thing: for a little while, you may *feel* like you've found a bit of peace. After all, if your church experience was as tumultuous as mine, you're probably more than relieved to be out of there. In my case, for a good stretch of time, there wasn't a single part of me that wanted to go back—to *any* church at all. While I think on some level I knew that my heart would never find rest outside of Jesus and the faith I'd turned my back on, I wasn't about to admit it.

That peace you're out there chasing through countless people and things is waiting for you in Christ. It exists nowhere else. You will not know joy until you feel the heart-bursting fulfillment that only comes from walking in the purpose and identity God has for you. Regardless of how many years you've spent running, there is a time and purpose for every season. Isn't it time to come home and watch God turn ruins into redemption?

Willing and Waiting

One of my most treasured parables in the Bible is the parable of the prodigal son. Luke 15:20 says, "While he was still a long way off, his father saw him and was filled with compassion for him; he ran to his son, threw his arms around him and kissed him" (NIV). This is the story's climax for me because scripture illustrates not only that God is willing to take us back after we have strayed but that *He's waiting for us.*

If you or I were to imagine ourselves in the shoes of the prodigal son, we'd likely envision God begrudgingly taking us back and loving us out of obligation. Thankfully, nothing could be further from the truth. When we take off running, God never stops scanning the road, waiting for our return.

We may think that we must clean up our act before returning to our Savior, but God has no such expectations. It's when we accept His love that we're made clean. He is the God who makes all things new, including you and me. He just *wants* us. And when that relationship is broken, He longs to restore it.

Seeking Restoration

In the parable of the lost sheep, Jesus told of a shepherd (Himself) who left his other ninety-nine sheep just to find one. I see this same act of restoration demonstrated in Peter's story. After denying he knew Jesus three times prior to the crucifixion, Peter wept bitterly. When we're actively distancing ourselves from Christ, it hurts. Inevitably, it's going to cause us grief. But, as in Peter's case, if we're still breathing, there's still an opportunity for reconciliation.

After Jesus's crucifixion, John 21 tells us that some of the disciples went fishing. When Jesus appeared on the shore and asked if they'd caught anything for breakfast, they admitted they hadn't had any luck. Knowing their plight, Jesus told the disciples to throw their net on the other side of the boat. Immediately, their net was filled with so many fish they didn't have the strength to pull it in. Realizing the man on shore was none other than Jesus, one of the disciples called out, "It's the Master!" Hearing this, Peter jumped into the shallow water and made his way to his Savior.

Peter, who'd once willingly turned his back on Jesus, *had* to be the first to get to Him. He was desperate for a restored relationship with the Savior He loved. And God, in His goodness, did not withhold restoration from Peter, just as He refuses to withhold it from us. No matter what we've done or how far we've fallen, we're never too far gone to return home.

Every road, every detour, has led you to this moment. Perhaps you're where I was twenty years ago, asking God, *Why didn't You protect me? Why didn't You save me from their hands? Why is this my story?* I'm here to tell you a day will come when the promise in Jeremiah 29:11 finally rings true for you: "I know the plans I have for you, . . .

plans for welfare and not for evil, to give you a future and a hope."

God's plans for your life are bigger and better than you can fathom. While you may not be able to see it now, one day you'll look back and see that God's hand was always there.

For the Good

"And we know that God causes everything to work together for the good of those who love God and are called according to his purpose for them" (Romans 8:28 NLT). Am I the only one who has continually tripped over this verse and hated the flippant use of it, as if it neatly explained and excused every tragedy we've ever experienced? In my life, this scripture was used more often than not to invalidate the abuse. It took years, but I finally discovered the promise this verse held: that my momentary pain would have eternal purpose.

Throughout the process of working on this book, I faced a dark and heavy season. I continually struggled with the concept of this verse as I waited for the "my good" part to come to pass. It took God doing a deep work in my heart to realize that when He says He works things for the good, it's not *just* for our good. It's also for the good of those crossing our paths, whether we meet them today or ten years from now. Just as Joseph's story demonstrated, there's a greater good in the bigger picture that we can't see in our moments of suffering. Suffering may never *feel* good, but that doesn't mean it's not producing good things *in* us that God will use for good *through* us.

If you'd asked me whether what I was going through would ever have a divine purpose when I was in a psych ward, on suicide watch, cutting my wrists, and overdosing on pills, I probably would have laughed in your face. As far as I knew, my story wouldn't end in anything but disaster. Nothing anyone could have said during those seasons of my life could have convinced me that God would one day use any of it for good. It was a journey Jesus had to take me on to reach a conclusion only He could lead me to.

I can't begin to describe the moments of awe and reverence I've experienced in recent years as I've watched God take the things born in my pit and my prison and use them for countless ministry opportunities, including this book. I have repeatedly sat in awe as God's taken what the enemy meant for evil and turned it into a redemptive purpose only He could pull off (Genesis 50:20). I would have been deprived of so much joy and robbed of doing anything good in this world if I had been successful in my suicide attempts. I will always be thankful for God's hand in preserving my life, even when I didn't want Him to.

Bind My Wandering Heart to Thee

Together, we've unraveled, sorted out, and dismantled many false beliefs that perhaps kept us from God and His people. Now that you've almost finished this book, have you found that your view of Jesus is accurate, or is it simply a projection of the people who hurt you?

For decades, I viewed all of Christianity through a lens of wounding. Until I healed from that, I didn't have a healthy view of church, Christians, or Christ. Once I separated Jesus from His followers' actions and allowed Him to faithfully show me His heart and character, I was able to meet Him in an authentic, meaningful way. How about you? Are you willing to take the same risk I did and consider how the real Jesus may radically differ from the version of Him that lives in your head right now?

In Exodus 20:18-20, God's people begged Moses to continue mediating between them and God. But there was a big problem with their request. Instead of entering into a relationship with God and discovering His character, the Israelites continued holding on to misconceptions about God that weren't rooted in truth because they didn't *know* Him. Like the Israelites in the desert, my pain and my false beliefs about God kept me running away from Him. Yet I can look back and tell you there wasn't one day when He wasn't faithful to pursue me. I just had to decide: was I willing to finally stop wandering and allow Him to restore all that was broken within me and in our relationship?

God never calls us to live in shame. He offers freedom from the condemnation that the enemy utilizes to keep us stuck and isolated. God isn't the one who hurt you. But He is the One who will walk you through every painful moment of healing. His love endures. It never ends. It reaches into the darkness and illuminates it.

If there's one thing I hope you walk away with as you close this book, it's that Jesus has never stopped loving you. He's seen all the places you've been. He knows why you ran. He understands the pain you've been trying to escape. He's sat with you in every dark moment. He's followed you all the days of your life. No matter where you have journeyed, He's been pursuing your heart as He faithfully waits for your return.

Have you ever wondered why God put Himself through this? Why does He pursue us when we curse and reject Him? Why does He leave the steadfast in the fold to come after our wandering hearts? Why is He still faithful when we are so faithless? Why would He endure rejection after rejection, yet *never* give up on us? The answer is simply love. Hebrews 12:2 says, "He was willing to die a shameful death on the cross because of the joy he knew would be his afterwards" (TLB). And what is His joy, what is His delight? It's you!

Your creator has gone to every length to capture your heart and restore you to the family of God. You are never so lost that you cannot be found, and you can never go somewhere His grace can't reach you. I know what it's like to test God, and I realize that perhaps our running is rooted on a subconscious level, as we attempt to see how far His love will stretch. *Does He still love me now? What about now?* Regardless of your reason for running, I can tell you that yes, even now—even after everything you've said and done to separate yourself from God—He never stopped waiting for you.

When I finally met Jesus, I realized that He didn't want my perfection. He wanted my heart. He didn't want me to hide all my broken pieces behind a phony smile on Sunday morning. He wanted the real me. He wasn't waiting to strike me with a lightning bolt at the first sign of a misstep on my behalf. He wasn't even mad at me. He loved me before time began. Even when I cursed Him and denied His existence in my darkest moments, He loved me. I had turned my back on Him, but He never turned away from me.

If you've pulled a Jonah when it comes to being a pro at running from God, I hope you'll pause long enough to see that the running has only kept you numb and weary. The peace, rest, and freedom we seek are solely found at our Savior's feet. Our souls cannot and will not be satisfied outside of a relationship with Jesus. We'll never truly be living our purpose until we are found in Him, because that's where all truth, significance, and meaning originates.

It's time to rebuild on a foundation of God and His truth. It's time to come home and run into the open arms of your Father. His love is endless, and His grace is enough. The gospel message has always begun with, "For God so loved the world . . ." (John 3:16). Nowhere does scripture say, "Except you, the one wrestling with depression. Except you, the one crippled by anxiety. Except you, the one battling suicidal thoughts." Even if another Christian placed a limitation on God's love for you, they don't have the authority to combat the red-letter words spoken in Matthew 19:14: "Let the little children come to me and do not hinder them." God's Word promises in John 6:37 that when you come running to Jesus, He holds on and doesn't let go. He will never turn you away, and no one on this earth has the right or power to stand between you and the cross.

And friend, I'll be one of the many cheering on the sidelines when you decide to come back to Jesus and I see you start coming down the road.

Jesus and Therapy

Jesus

At the end of chapter eight, I asked you to write down which moments ultimately drove you away from Christianity and Christ. Now that those experiences have been acknowledged, it may be time to burn that list. None of us wants to live as if the wounds inflicted on us are more significant than the wounding that Jesus endured on the cross. While your time of processing your past may last for years to come, today you get to choose whether or not you're willing to step back into the waiting arms of your Savior. Pray this prayer with me:

Dear Heavenly Father,
Thank You for Your promise to never leave or forsake me. Thank You that nothing can separate me from Your love. Though I've wandered, You've been faithful to pursue me. You've never given up hope that I'd return home. Will You begin to restore my heart and bind up my wounds? Show me where I still need to heal, what I need to release, and where You want me to be planted in this season of my life. Allow my roots to grow deep, with You as my foundation. I commit myself to following You and You alone. I surrender my life into Your loving hands, knowing there is no safer place for me. Thank You, Lord, for welcoming me home. In Jesus's name. Amen.

Therapy

Even though we are coming to the end of this book, our healing journey isn't over. Part of walking with the Lord means we'll always be in progress. With each new layer peeled back or each new twist in life's road, He'll make us more and more like Himself, and we'll get closer to a healthier version of ourselves. Where do you see yourself a year from now? Five years from now? Discuss these goals with your therapist and create a road map of what you must work on to achieve those milestones. As you take the necessary steps forward, remember that healing and growth are always possible with Jesus by your side. One day at a time, my friend. Your future self will be so proud that you didn't give up.

Final Thoughts from Tabitha

If you picked up *Jesus and Therapy* out of a desire to be an ally and advocate for the mental health community, I'm thrilled you're here. The church desperately needs people like you who want to effect change in the body of Christ by raising awareness about mental health.

Here are some brief ways you can meaningfully engage with the people in your church, community, friend group, or family:

- **Educate yourself.** Broaden your understanding of mental health issues by reading, listening to podcasts, and engaging in conversations. Rather than adding to the stigma around getting professional help, create a list of qualified mental health professionals and resources that you can recommend. By doing so, you are demonstrating the normality of mental health care and helping to reduce the shame associated with seeking it.

- **Create a safe place.** If you have or are currently walking through mental health struggles, speak up about your struggle or your testimony. That brave step of vulnerability will create a safe space for others to share their struggles. Authenticity breeds authenticity.

- **Love others where they are.** The church is meant to be a hospital for the broken, not a museum for shiny, happy saints. Loving people exactly where they are means patiently rooting for them in their healing journeys and asking how you can show up for them in tangible ways. When you willingly meet others where they are, you become a living example of Christ's faithfulness to stay when others walk away.

- **Raise awareness.** Normalize mental health discussions, especially if you're in a position of leadership or influence. It's crucial for believers to see examples of capable and intelligent people doing great things in the world while actively fighting for their mental health and that of their church family. If the church's view of mental health struggles is limited to the equivalent of a psychiatric ward, we're in trouble. While a few might wear their scars for all the world to see, many capable and intelligent people doing extraordinary things in the world fight this invisible battle daily. Both groups need to know they're welcome and that they're not alone.

- **Be an advocate.** Ask your church if they will host mental health awareness training sessions for their leadership. Organizations like Mental Health Grace Alliance, Speak Out PDX, and others offer these life-changing resources.

God delights in giving us opportunities to minister to others. Take time to become equipped and educated regarding mental health issues. Then, if you're willing, He'll use you as a lighthouse for those attempting to navigate life's murky waters—whether you've waded through them before or not. Remember, God is not limited by you. He is perfectly capable of operating through your weaknesses and using you to speak hope to others.

Author's Note

To each and every one of you who did me the honor of coming on this journey with me, thank you. Thank you for creating space for me to share my story and welcoming me into your lives throughout this book. I cannot wait to see all God has in store for you and hear how He's using you for His Kingdom.

With every turn of the page, I hope you find yourself one step closer to knowing that Jesus and therapy go hand in hand in the journey to emotional well-being. True healing can be found when we couple our faith in Jesus with the bravery needed to ask for help from the comforters, advocates, and wise counselors He's generously placed in our path.

Cheering you on,

Tabitha

Acknowledgments

This book has been in the making for a long time, and I could not have sent my story out to the world without an incredible team supporting me.

I also couldn't have gotten this far without my incredible agent, Marisa Zeppieri-Caruana. Marisa: God brought you along when I needed you most. From start to finish, you fought for this book and believed in it when I couldn't. You have become a precious friend, and I will forever be indebted to you for going on this journey with me.

To my publisher, Dexterity: You saw the value in this message and invested in me as a first-time author, and I'm eternally grateful for this experience. Thank you for giving me this opportunity to deliver my message to a broader audience than I ever could on my own! My thanks especially to Matt West for being so invested in this book and the creative process.

To my sweet editor, Melanie McGaughey: Thank you for coming alongside me and helping me craft these words into precisely what they should be. I can never express my complete gratitude for how you advocated for me, supported me, and cheered me on during the editing process. You are the best editor a girl could ask for, and you were a pleasure to work with. I'd like to give a special shoutout to Janna Walkup and Elisa Stanford for their editing contributions as well.

To Kayla Johnson: The good Lord knows there *wouldn't* have been a book without your faithful influence in my life. You've spoken the truth when I desperately needed to hear it. You've repeatedly affirmed the path God has placed before me. You've picked me up countless times when I couldn't stand in the fire anymore. You've loved me when I felt unlovable and too broken to be used by God. You've shown me the Father's heart again and again. I know Jesus more deeply because of you. "Thank you" will never be enough for being such a rock for me. I love you dearly and cherish every time we speak.

To my Sister-Friends—Amber, Elizabeth, Jessika, and Jennifer: Y'all have been there for all the tears, all the breaking, and every high and low. After every no, you'd remind me that one day I'd get a yes. You each have lifted me up in fervent prayers in my most desperate moments, and I'm not quite sure how I lived before we became friends. I love y'all so much and am so thankful I get to do life with you.

To all the friends who showed up for me, prayed for me, and sent messages to check on me: You have lifted my head and held me up more times than I can count. I will never forget the ones who stood by me through this extraordinary journey. Thank you to Danielle P., Lisa L., Caris S., Jennifer N., Tasha S., Courtney D., Mona S., and so many others who have surrounded me with love during this time.

To Kehau and Mimi: You were my lifelines at different points in my childhood and sources of strength and stability that I desperately clung to when nothing else made sense. For all the hours, prayers, and love that you both have invested in my life, I will never forget your kindness.

To my children—Caitlyn, Christian, and Colton: All I ever set out to do in my life was to love you well, show you Jesus, and give you a childhood you wouldn't have to recover from. You each have inspired me every day to never stop chasing healing. I love you all more than life. You had to ride out this rocky road of seeing this book to completion. You cheered me on when blessings were flowing, and you buckled up and held tight to me and Jesus when the fiery arrows started to fly. You are the most amazing kids anyone could ask for, and you will always be the best thing that's ever happened to me.

To Matt: Thank you for believing that I was called to do this and for being willing to bend so I could chase after all that Jesus asked of me. More times than I can count, you've held down the fort so I could write, heal, and be poured out again. You challenged me not to throw in the towel when I had nothing left to give, and you encouraged me not to give in to despair when life crushed me on every side. Thank you for never wavering in your support of this mission.

To the family who has stood by me, celebrated with me, loved me through the hard times, and supported me following God's lead on this: Thank you.

To my first therapist, Dr. G, and my last therapist, Norma: You were God's hands and feet in the longest, most drawn-out valleys of my life. One of you helped me make it out alive so that the other could walk with me through the pain I had to process on the other side. Each of you made a tremendous difference in my life and helped shape the person I am today. I will always be grateful.

To my Redeemed Mama Community: Sharing this story with you was so important to me because this book belongs to all of us. You've supported me and the testimony God has given me since day one. Every message, prayer, and comment of encouragement has lifted me through more than you know. You've fought the good fight with me and basically prayed this book into reality. I hope reading it reaffirms how precious you are to Jesus and brings you the healing and peace you deserve. I love you all.

To Palm Photography: Thank you so much for sharing your amazing gift of photography with me and providing me with beautiful headshot photos. I appreciate and love you both!

To Lisa Tomberlin: Thank you for taking the time to do my hair for headshots and always being the best hairstylist/therapist a girl could ask for!

And to Jesus: You have never let me go and have been so faithful to send me sign after sign that You've called me to do this. You have brought restoration and redemption to the most barren and broken places in my life, and I will count it my greatest honor to tell others what You've done for me for the rest of my days. Thank you for choosing me, equipping me, loving me, carrying me. You are a faithful and good God. All for your glory, Jesus.

Mental Health Resources

Mental Health Phone Numbers and Texts
- Suicide and Crisis Lifeline: 988
- Crisis Text Line: Text HOME to 741741
- National Alliance on Mental Illness: 1-800-950-NAMI (6264)
- Mental Health America (MHA): 1-800-969-6642
- National Maternal Mental Health Hotline: 1-833-TLC-MAMA (6262)
- SAFE (Self-Abuse Finally Ends) Information Line: 1-800-DONT-CUT (366-8288)
- Substance Abuse and Mental Health Services Administration (SAMHSA): 1-800-662-4357

Mental Health Websites
- Christian Counselor Directory: https://www.christiancounselordirectory.com
- Depression and Bipolar Support Alliance: https://www.dbsalliance.org
- Better Help: https://www.betterhelp.com
- American Chronic Pain Association: https://www.theacpa.org
- Veterans Crisis Line: https://www.veteranscrisisline.net

- Psychology Today:
  https://www.psychologytoday.com/us/therapists
- GoodTherapy.org:
  https://www.goodtherapy.org/find-therapist.html
- Suicide Prevention, Awareness, and Support:
  http://www.suicide.org
- Christian Mental Health Workshops:
  https://www.speakoutpdx.com

Mental Health Support Podcasts

- *The Unraveling* (kellibachara.com)
- *Renew* (renewfaithconference.com)
- *Fresh Hope for Mental Health*
  (freshhopeformentalhealth.com)
- *Thrive: Mental Health and the Art of Living Free*
  (melissaclarkcounseling.com)
- *Therapy and Theology*
  (lysaterkeurst.com/therapy-and-theology/)
- *CXMH: A Podcast on Faith and Mental Health*
  (cxmhpodcast.com)

Scriptural Affirmations

I am a child of the King.
But you are God's chosen treasure—priests who are kings, a spiritual "nation" set apart as God's devoted ones. He called you out of darkness to experience his marvelous light, and now he claims you as his very own.

  (1 Peter 2:9 TPT)

I am valuable.
For you know that God paid a ransom to save you from the empty life you inherited from your ancestors. And it was not paid with mere gold or silver, which lose their value. It was the precious blood of Christ, the sinless, spotless Lamb of God.

  (1 Peter 1:18-19 NLT)

I am chosen.
Even before he made the world, God loved us and chose us in Christ to be holy and without fault in his eyes.

  (Ephesians 1:4 NLT)

I am heard.
I am passionately in love with God because he
  listens to me.
He hears my prayers and answers them.
As long as I live I'll keep praying to him,
for he stoops down to listen to my heart's cry.

  (Psalm 116:1-2 TPT)

I am enough.
Everything we could ever need for life and godliness
has already been deposited in us by his divine
power. For all this was lavished upon us through the
rich experience of knowing him who has called us
by name and invited us to come to him through a
glorious manifestation of his goodness.
    (2 Peter 1:3 TPT)

I am not alone.
The LORD himself goes before you and will be with you;
he will never leave you nor forsake you.
    (Deuteronomy 31:8 NIV)

I am accepted.
You will bring God glory when you accept and
welcome one another as partners, just as the
Anointed One has fully accepted you and received
you as his partner.
    (Romans 15:7 TPT)

I am blameless.
[In His love] He chose us in Christ [actually selected
us for Himself as His own] before the foundation
of the world, so that we would be holy [that is,
consecrated, set apart for Him, purpose-driven] and
blameless in His sight.
    (Ephesians 1:4 AMP)

I am loved.
So now I live with the confidence that there is nothing in the universe with the power to separate us from God's love. I'm convinced that his love will triumph over death, life's troubles, fallen angels, or dark rulers in the heavens. There is nothing in our present or future circumstances that can weaken his love.
(Romans 8:38 TPT)

I am God's masterpiece.
We are God's masterpiece. He has created us anew in Christ Jesus, so we can do the good things he planned for us long ago.
(Ephesians 2:10 NLT)

Mental Health Self-Care Checklist

✓ Get adequate sleep

✓ Drink enough water

✓ Get out in nature

✓ Take prescribed meds as directed

✓ Stay connected

✓ Attend regularly scheduled counseling sessions

✓ Set small, attainable goals

✓ Try a relaxing activity

✓ Practice breathing techniques

✓ Journal

✓ Go for a walk

✓ Challenge your negative thought patterns

✓ Practice daily gratitude

✓ Try something new

✓ Make to-do lists to clear your mind

✓ Listen to an uplifting podcast or encouraging music

✓ Unplug from technology

✓ Take a mental health day

✓ Get a massage

✓ Avoid toxic people

✓ Practice saying no

✓ Communicate your needs

✓ Feed your body nourishing foods

- ✓ Develop self-soothing routines
- ✓ Join a support group
- ✓ Go on a day trip
- ✓ Find a reason to laugh
- ✓ Do something nice for yourself
- ✓ Practice mindfulness
- ✓ Be aware of self-talk
- ✓ Take time off of social media
- ✓ Purchase a weighted blanket
- ✓ Have a movie marathon
- ✓ Care for your daily hygiene
- ✓ Accept and validate your emotions
- ✓ Give yourself grace on the hard days
- ✓ Read a book
- ✓ Reach out for help

Mental Health Checkup

How do I know if I am struggling with my mental health?

Our mental health is a result of our genetics, our physical and social environments, chemical imbalances, diet, circumstances, and unresolved or ongoing trauma. Often referred to as a "mental health disorder," this illness can affect our behavior, mood, and thought patterns. A few examples of mental illness include anxiety disorders, mood disorders, eating disorders, addictive behaviors, personality disorders, psychotic disorders, and trauma- or stress-related disorders.

Though all of us have mental health concerns from time to time, a mental health concern can evolve into a mental illness when ongoing symptoms affect our ability to function on a day-to-day basis or cause frequent stress. If you are unsure if you or a loved one is suffering from a mental health condition, consider the following list. Reach out for help if either of you is experiencing several of these symptoms or any one of them to an extreme:

You may need to reach out for help if you are experiencing any of the following:

- Feelings of sadness or "being down"
- Confused thinking or reduced ability to concentrate
- Excessive fears or worries or extreme feelings of guilt
- Extreme mood changes of highs and lows
- Withdrawal from friends and activities
- Significant tiredness, low energy, or problems sleeping
- Detachment from reality (delusions), paranoia, or hallucinations

- Inability to cope with daily problems or stress
- Trouble understanding and relating to situations and people
- Problems with alcohol or drug use
- Major changes in eating habits
- Excessive anger, hostility, or violence
- Suicidal thinking

How do I know if I have depression?

Depression manifests itself in different ways depending on the person. If you've suffered from at least a few of the symptoms below for two weeks (or more), and they're interfering with your ability to sleep, work, study, or eat, you may be dealing with depression. There are different types of depression, from major depressive disorder to bipolar to manic depression and so on. While not intended to diagnose, the list of these symptoms may at least help you identify if a trip to a counselor is warranted by you or a loved one.

Possible symptoms of depression:

- Feelings of hopelessness or pessimism
- Persistent sad, anxious, or empty mood
- Feelings of irritability, frustration, or restlessness
- Feelings of guilt, worthlessness, or helplessness
- Loss of interest or pleasure in hobbies or activities
- Decreased energy, fatigue, or being "slowed down"
- Difficulty concentrating, remembering, or making decisions
- Difficulty sleeping, early morning awakening, or oversleeping

- Changes in appetite or unplanned weight changes
- Aches or pains, headaches, cramps, or digestive problems without a clear physical cause that do not ease with treatment
- Suicide attempts or thoughts of death or suicide

How can I tell if I suffer from anxiety?

Having an anxiety disorder isn't always associated with panic attacks, but for many, they come with the territory. In the midst of a panic attack, a person may feel a pounding or racing heart, experience sweating, trembling, or tingling, and may even suffer from chest pain. One may have a feeling of impending doom or of being completely out of control. Anxiety can be a constant feeling. Some people with anxiety remain outwardly calm and seemingly in control while their mind might be racing. Anxiety can be as simple as numbing out (dissociation or depersonalization) or feeling as if the worst thing you can imagine is about to happen. Living in that sense of fear and anticipation *all the time* is exhausting. If not addressed and treated, anxiety can interfere with and be downright detrimental to one's daily life.

Possible symptoms of generalized anxiety disorder:

- Feeling restless, wound up, or on edge
- Being easily fatigued
- Having difficulty concentrating
- Being irritable
- Having headaches, muscle aches, stomachaches, or unexplained pain
- Having difficulty controlling feelings of worry
- Having problems falling asleep or staying asleep

Notes

1. "Understanding Disorders: What Are Anxiety and Depression?" ADAA, updated October 25, 2022, https://adaa.org/understanding-anxiety.

2. Mental Health Disorder Statistics," Johns Hopkins Medicine, accessed November 15, 2024, https://www.hopkinsmedicine.org/health/wellness-and-prevention/mental-health-disorder-statistics/.

3. Kati Blocker, "Understanding suicidal ideation and how to help," UC Health, May 24, 2021, https://www.uchealth.org/today/suicidal-ideation-and-how-to-help/.

4. Shishira Sreenivas and Stephanie Langmaid, "What Is Suicidal Ideation?" WebMD, January 18, 2024, https://www.webmd.com/mental-health/suicidal-ideation/.

5. "2023 NSDUH Annual National Report," SAMHSA, July 30, 2024, https://www.samhsa.gov/data/report/2023-nsduh-annual-national-report/.

6. Mental Health and Suicide," Psychology Today, accessed November 15, 2024, https://www.psychologytoday.com/us/basics/suicide/mental-health-conditions-suicide/.

7. Marcia Purse, "Understanding Suicidal Ideation and Ways to Cope," Verywell Mind, Updated September 24, 2024, https://www.verywellmind.com/suicidal-ideation-380609/.

8. "Suicide," NIMH, https://www.nimh.nih.gov/health/statistics/suicide/.

9. Ben Kesslen, "Megachurch pastor Jarrid Wilson, known for his mental health advocacy, dies by suicide," *NBC News*, September 11, 2019, https://www.nbcnews.com/news/us-news/megachurch-pastor-jarrid-wilson-known-his-mental-health-advocacy-dies-n1052301/.

10. Kayla Stoecklein (@kaylasteck), "Last night, the love of my life, the father of my children and the pastor of our incredible church took his last breath and went to be with Jesus," Instagram, August 26, 2018, https://www.instagram.com/p/Bm8wJ6XH397/.

11. Michael Cooper, "6 Keys for Pastors in Maintaining Mental Health," Lifeway Research, May 14, 2019, https://research.lifeway.com/2019/05/14/6-keys-for-pastors-in-maintaining-mental-health/.

12. Ibid.

13. "13 Stats on Mental Health and the Church," Lifeway Research, May 1, 2018, https://research.lifeway.com/2018/05/01/13-stats-on-mental-health-and-the-church/.

14. Understanding psychotherapy and how it works APA, updated December 12, 2023, https://www.apa.org/topics/psychotherapy/understanding/.

15. Ashley Olvine, "What Are the Different Types and Benefits of Therapy?" Verywell Health, updated August 1, 2024, https://www.verywellhealth.com/benefits-of-therapy-5219732.

16. Bessel van der Kolk, *The Body Keeps the Score: Brain, Mind, and Body in the Healing of Trauma* (New York: Penguin Books, 2015).

17. "Depressive disorder (depression)," WHO, March 31, 2023, https://www.who.int/news-room/fact-sheets/detail/depression/.

18. "Cognitive Behavioral Therapy (CBT)," GoodTherapy, updated June 5, 2018, https://www.goodtherapy.org/learn-about-therapy/types/cognitive-behavioral-therapy/.

19. "What is EMDR Therapy? For Laypeople," EMDR Institute, https://www.emdr.com/what-is-emdr/.

20. Dr. Adam Bletsoe, "Sometimes Healing Feels Like Breaking at First," https://dradambletsoe.com/sometimes-healing-feels-like-breaking-at-first/.

21. Joyce Meyer has stated this a few different ways, such as in "How Do I Forgive?" https://www.identitynetwork.net/Articles-and-Prophetic-Words/.

About the Author

Tabitha Yates is a mental health advocate, writer, and suicide attempt survivor known as *The Redeemed Mama* on social media, where she writes about faith, mental health, and God's redemptive plan. Tabitha's writing has been featured in *Yahoo News, MSN, Relevant Magazine, The Mighty*, and *Love What Matters*, with more to come. Through practical advice, personal anecdotes, and biblical insights, Tabitha uses her platform to help renew the faith of millions of individuals struggling with where their faith and mental health intersect.

Tabitha is the daughter and granddaughter of military veterans, having lived in California, Iceland, Guam, and Hawaii by the age of eight. She and her husband, a now-retired Army officer, have lived all over the United States. They and their three children now call the Tucson, Arizona, area home. *Jesus and Therapy: Bridging the Gap between Faith and Mental Health* is her first book.

You can find more of Tabitha's writing on her website, theredeemedmama.com. Follow her on social media for daily interactions and encouragement.

Helpful. Hopeful. Inspiring.

Books that make the world a better place.

Dexterity is an award-winning, proudly independent publisher producing books that inspire and help people get where they want to go. Check out these books and more at www.DexterityBooks.com.

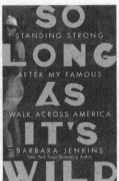

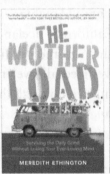

In a book club?

Download our discussion guides at store.dexteritybooks.com/pages/bookclubs.

Follow Dexterity on social media: @DexterityBooks

Join our email list for contests previews, and more.